AVON FREE PUBLIC LIBRARY
281 COUNTRY CLUB ROAD, AVON, CT 06001

FAREWELL, BRINDAVOINE

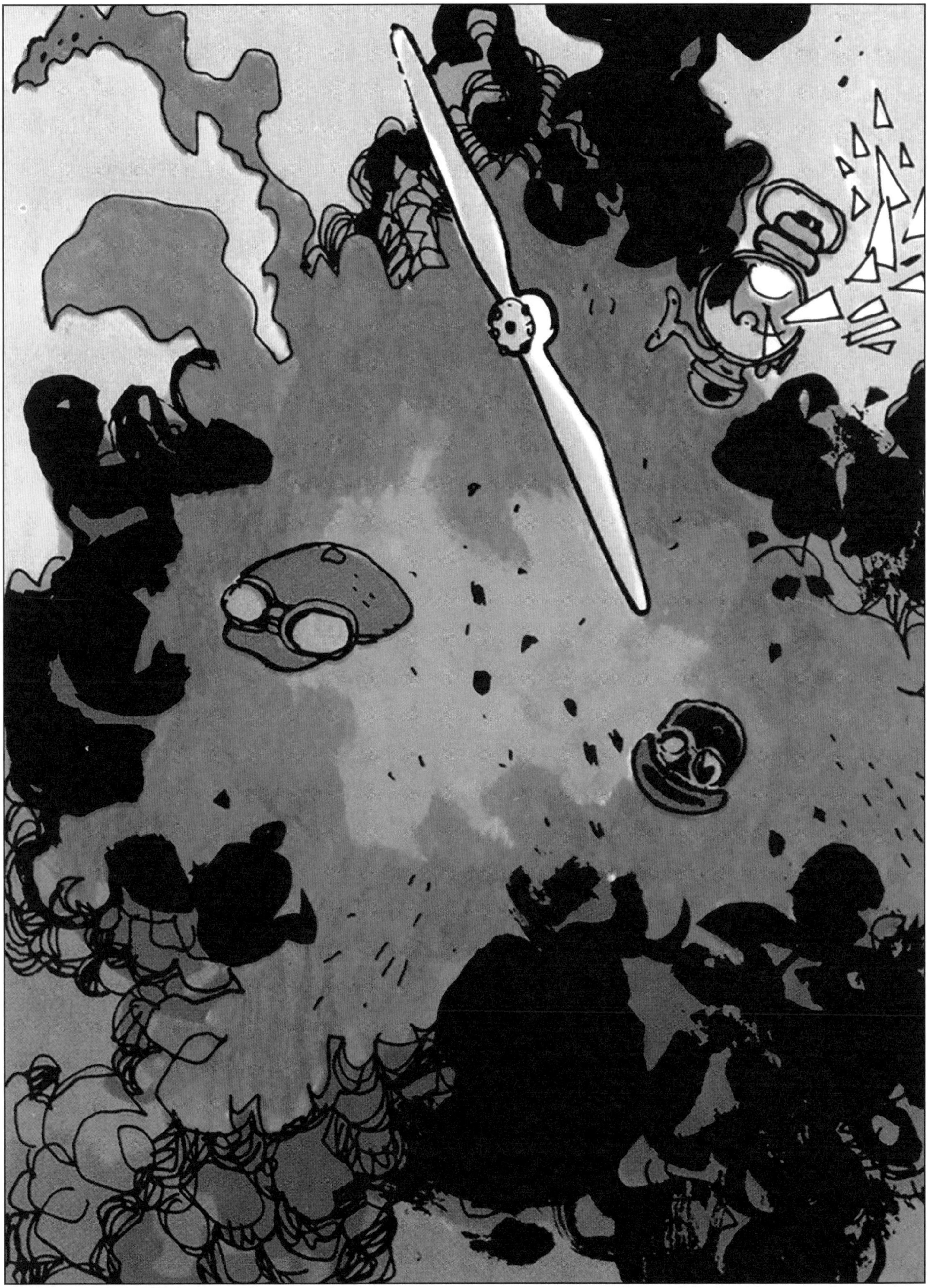

TARDI

FAREWELL, BRINDAVOINE

Translated by Jenna Allen

GRAPHIC
TAR
col

AVON FREE PUBLIC LIBRARY
281 COUNTRY CLUB ROAD, AVON CT 06001

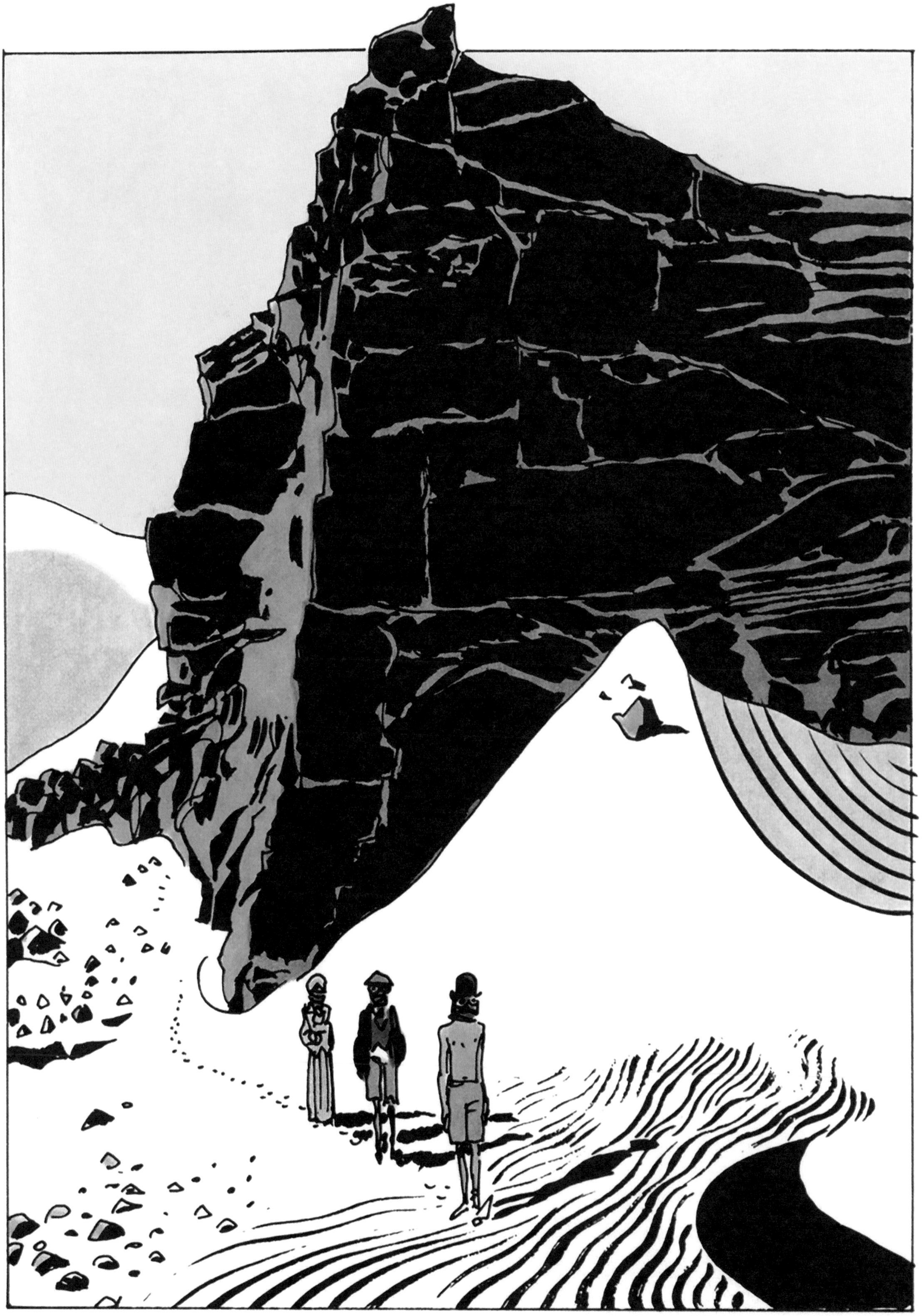

PREFACE

AN AUTHOR'S EARLY WORK often reveals certain obsessions and antipathies that will mark their entire oeuvre. Published in the weekly French comics magazine *Pilote* between 1972 and 1973, Tardi's stories collected in this volume don't have plots in the traditional sense. Rather, they're a succession of spectacular visual sequences that follow the surrealistic logic of dreams and nightmares.

Tardi's anachronistic imagery borrows from Albert Robida's futuristic illustrations, Jules Verne's extraordinary adventures, and Louis Feuillade's silent film serials *Judex* and *Fantômas*. His illustrations prefigure the emergence of steampunk by almost 10 years, with his Eiffel Tower-inspired architecture, airplanes, zeppelins, steam-powered engines, starched frock coats, and floppy hats.

Lucien Brindavoine is a dandy, a photographer, a pacifist, an anarchist, and an utter scoundrel. In a way, he resembles the dilletante character of Jean des Esseintes in Joris-Karl Huysmans' decadent novel, *Against Nature*. You can see the resemblance in his mansion's bizarre décor and his jaded, impassive personality. But the plot twists and dramatic turns that Tardi inflicts on his scoundrel much more resemble the outlandish intrigues of Gaston Leroux, creator of *Phantom of the Opera* and Detective Rouletabille.

You can detect these allusions and more in Tardi's *Adèle Blanc-Sec* series (which may be considered a sequel to this volume, insofar as Brindavoine appears in it), as well as his epic tales of the Great War, *It Was the War of the Trenches* and *Goddamn This War!*. Open your eyes wide: this chaotic, topsy-turvy world of the modernist 19th century will not survive the atrocities of World War I! Nevertheless, it continues to haunt the global comic scene...

Happy reading!

—Benoît Mouchart

Editorial Director of Graphic Novels at Casterman
2021

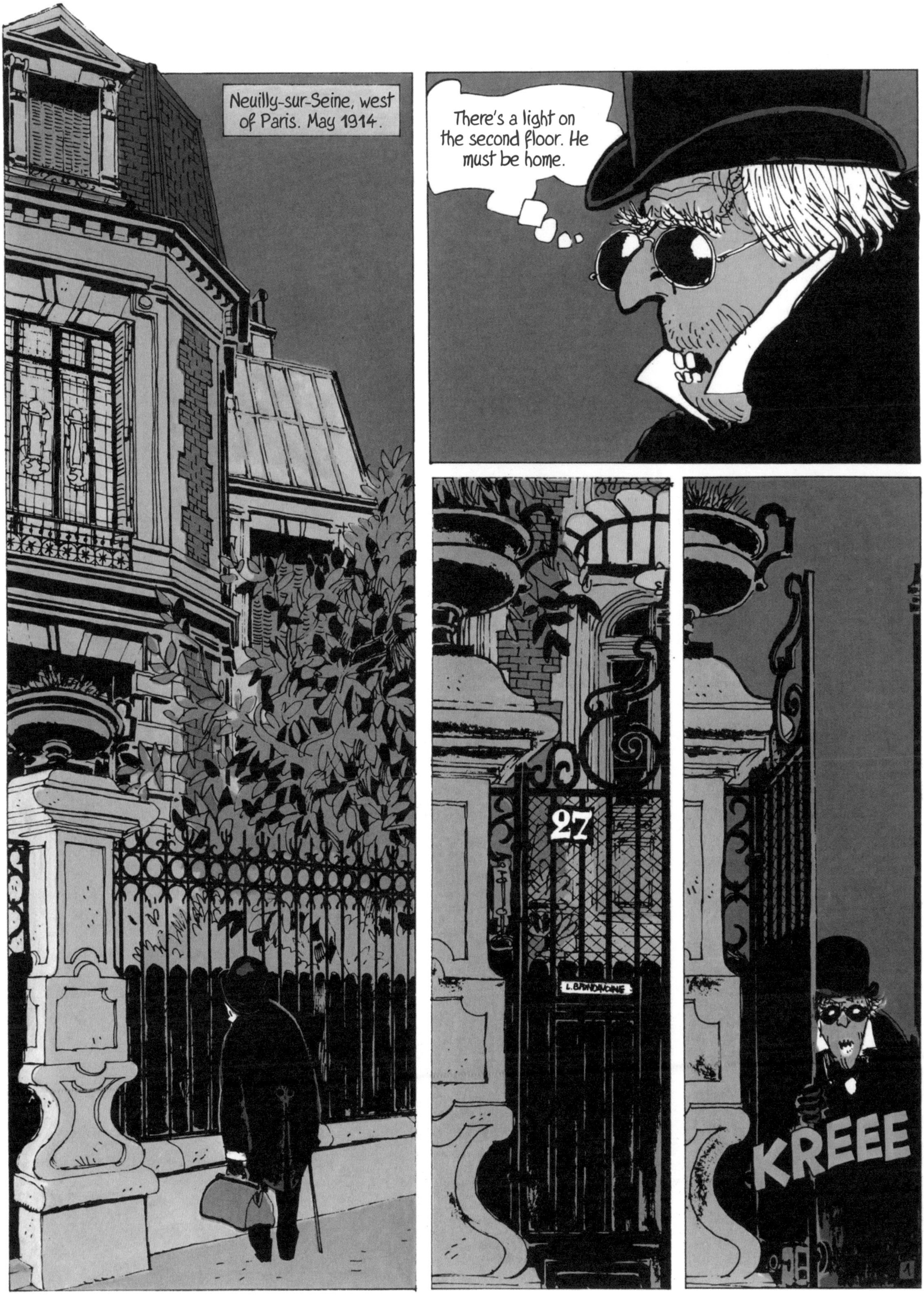

Neuilly-sur-Seine, west of Paris. May 1914.
There's a light on the second floor. He must be home.
27
KREEE

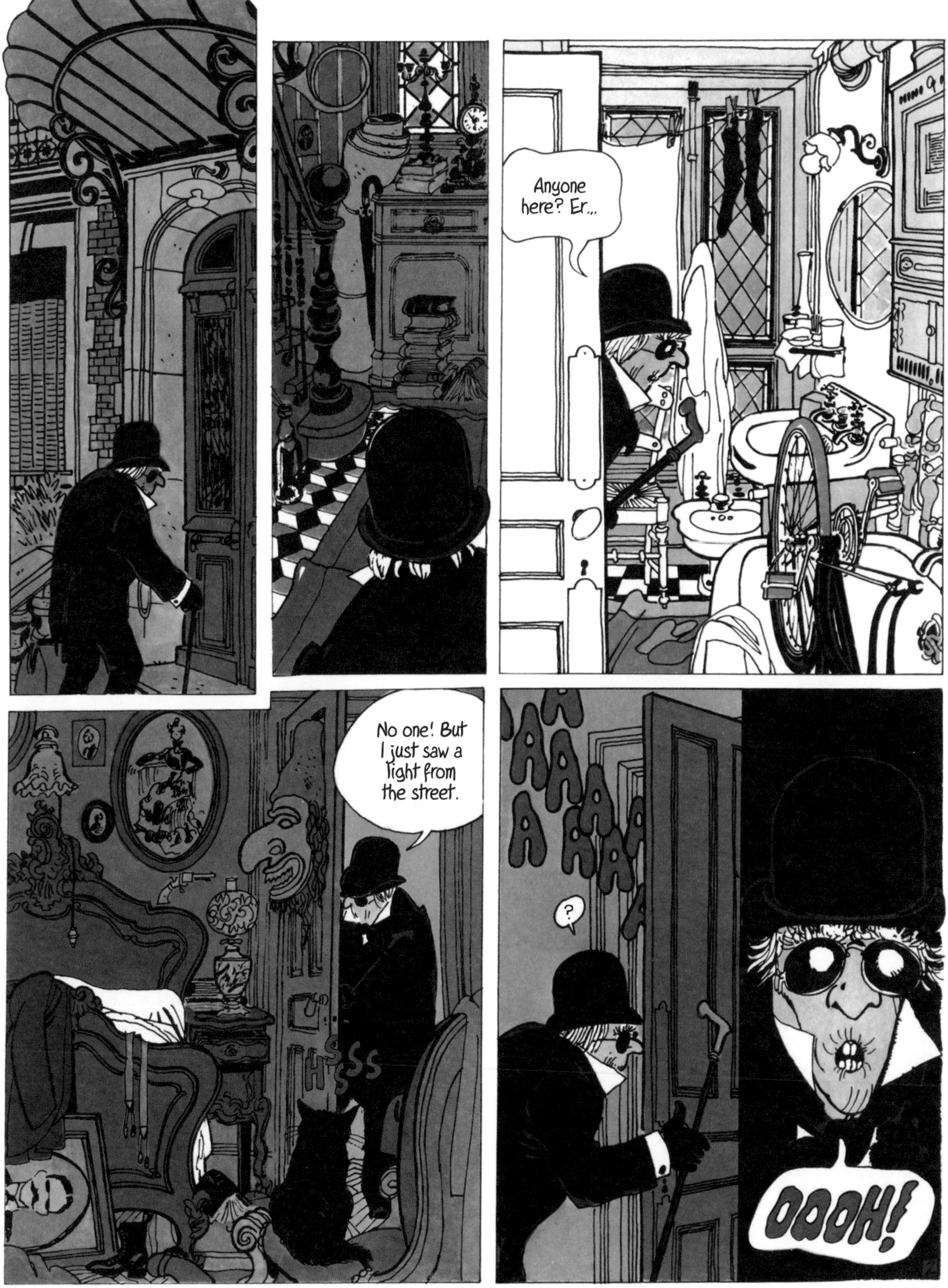
Anyone here? Er...
No one! But I just saw a light from the street.
HSSS
?
OOOH!

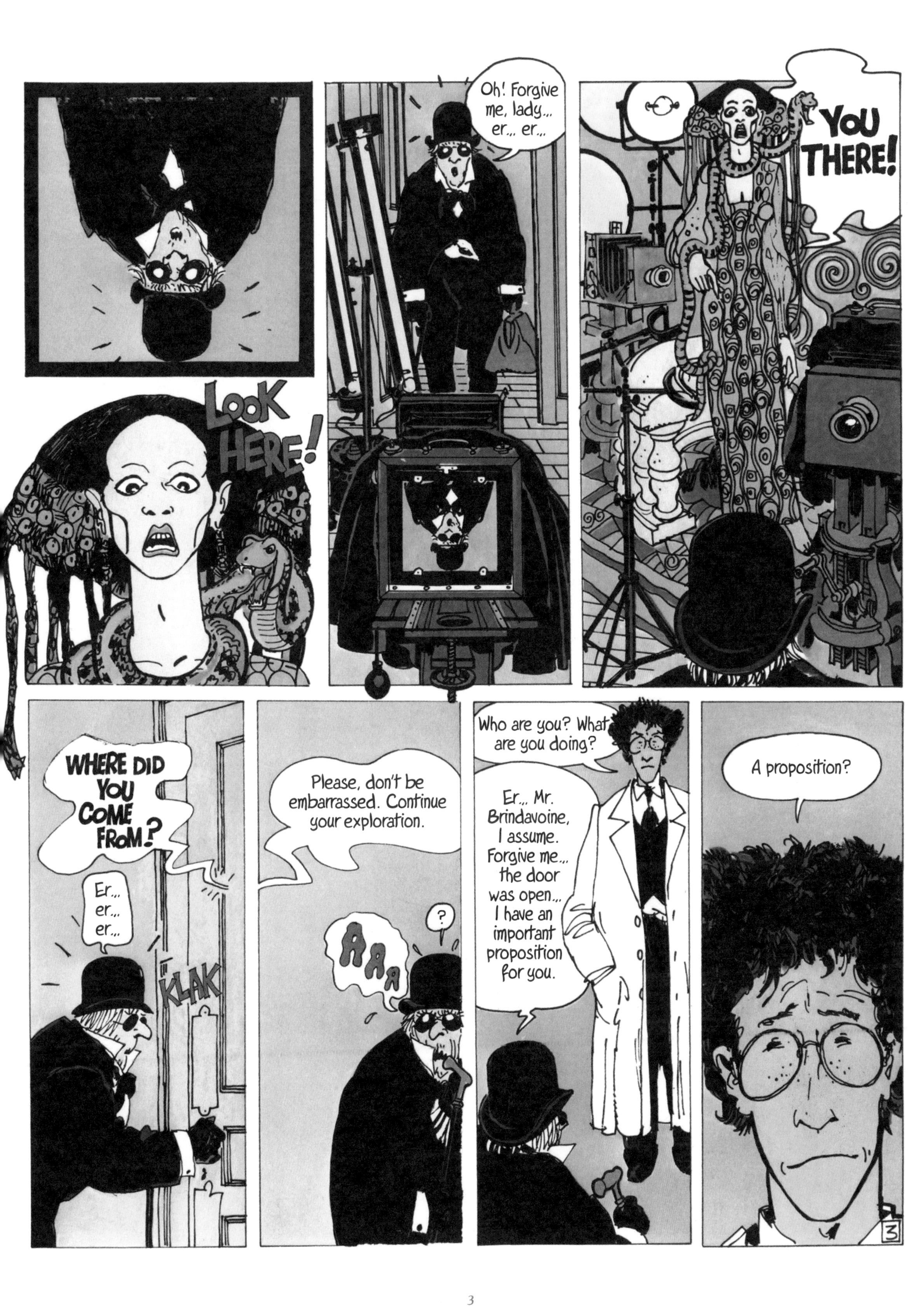
Oh! Forgive me, lady... er... er...
YOU THERE!
LOOK HERE!
WHERE DID YOU COME FROM?
Er... er... er...
KLAK
Please, don't be embarrassed. Continue your exploration.
AAA
?
Who are you? What are you doing?
Er... Mr. Brindavoine, I assume. Forgive me... the door was open... I have an important proposition for you.
A proposition?
3

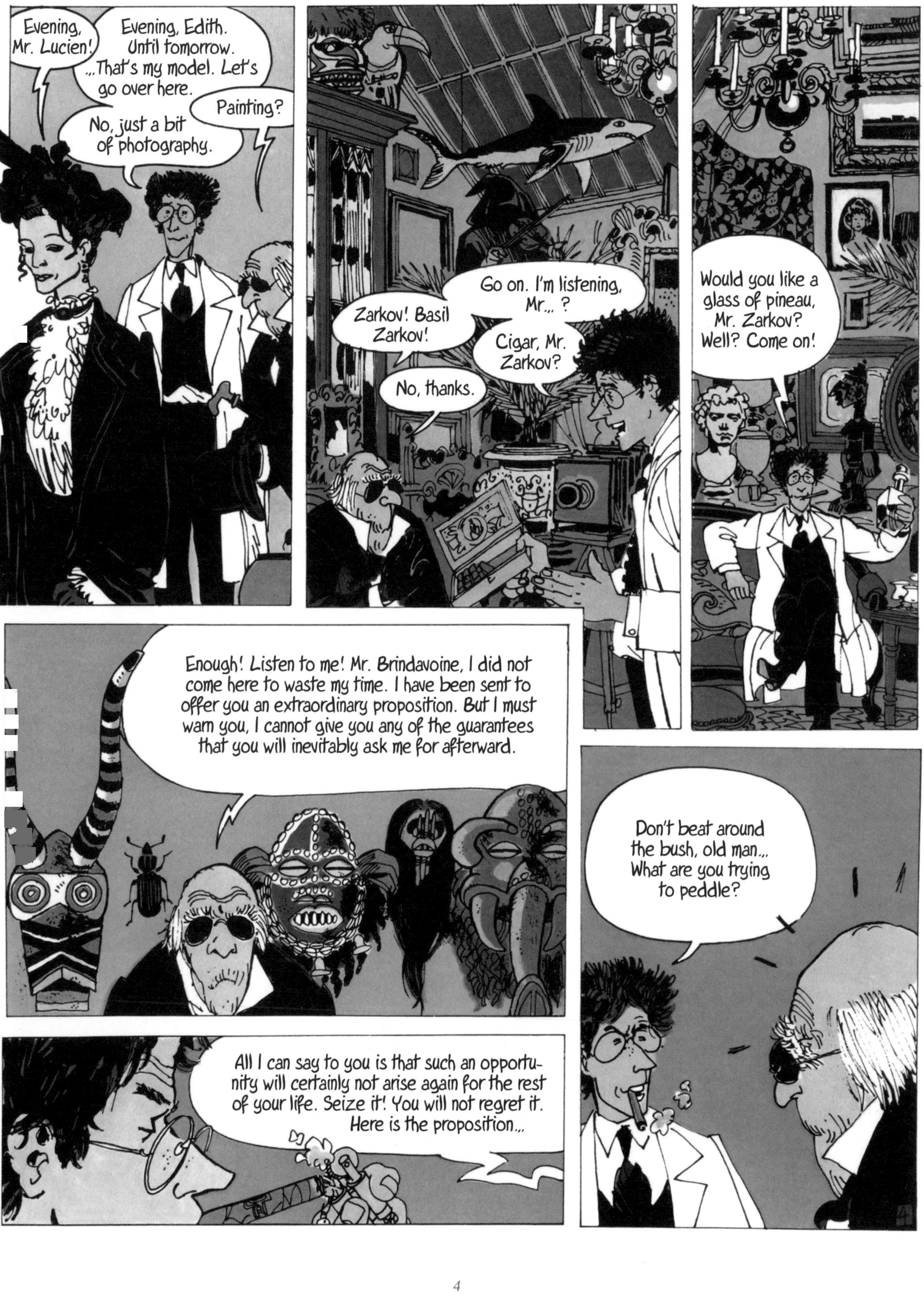
Evening, Mr. Lucien!
Evening, Edith. Until tomorrow. ...That's my model. Let's go over here.
Painting?
No, just a bit of photography.
Zarkov! Basil Zarkov!
Go on. I'm listening, Mr... ?
Cigar, Mr. Zarkov?
No, thanks.
Would you like a glass of pineau, Mr. Zarkov? Well? Come on!
Enough! Listen to me! Mr. Brindavoine, I did not come here to waste my time. I have been sent to offer you an extraordinary proposition. But I must warn you, I cannot give you any of the guarantees that you will inevitably ask me for afterward.
Don't beat around the bush, old man... What are you trying to peddle?
All I can say to you is that such an opportunity will certainly not arise again for the rest of your life. Seize it! You will not regret it. Here is the proposition...

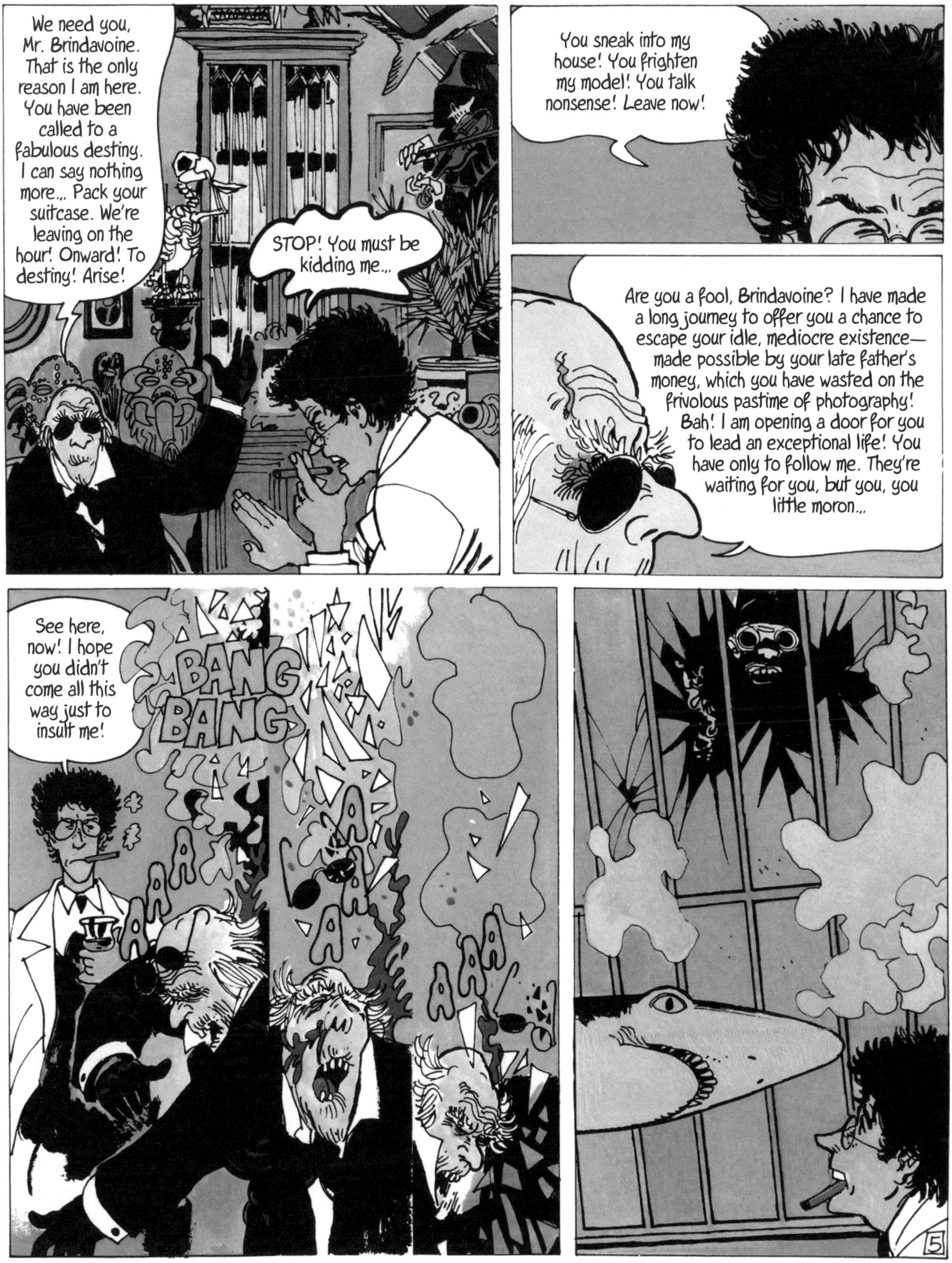

We need you, Mr. Brindavoine. That is the only reason I am here. You have been called to a fabulous destiny. I can say nothing more... Pack your suitcase. We're leaving on the hour! Onward! To destiny! Arise!
STOP! You must be kidding me...
You sneak into my house! You frighten my model! You talk nonsense! Leave now!
Are you a fool, Brindavoine? I have made a long journey to offer you a chance to escape your idle, mediocre existence—made possible by your late father's money, which you have wasted on the frivolous pastime of photography! Bah! I am opening a door for you to lead an exceptional life! You have only to follow me. They're waiting for you, but you, you little moron...
See here, now! I hope you didn't come all this way just to insult me!
BANG BANG
AAAA
AAAA
AAAA
5

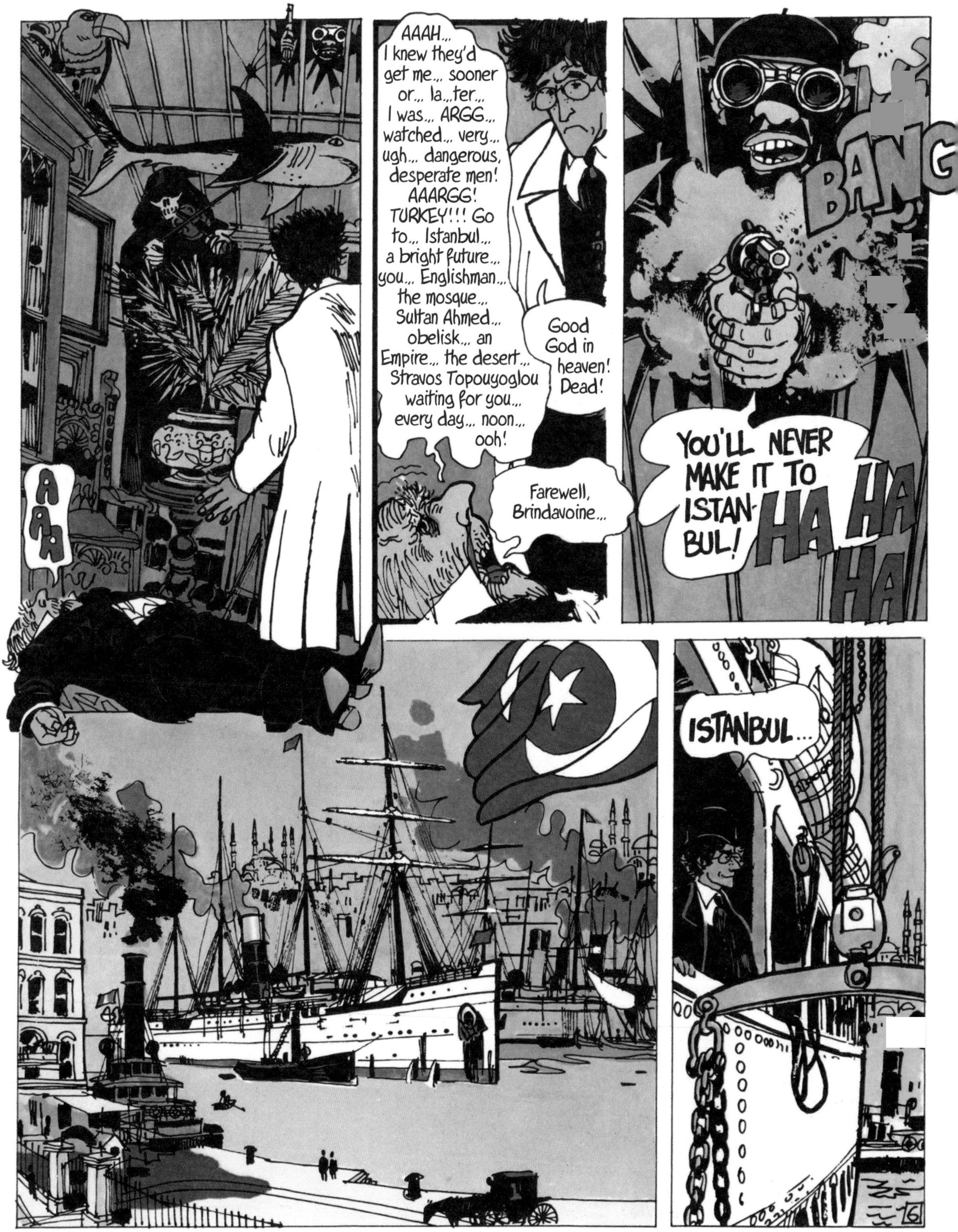
AAAH... I knew they'd get me... sooner or... la...ter... I was... ARGG... watched... very... ugh... dangerous, desperate men! AAARGG! TURKEY!!! Go to... Istanbul... a bright future... you... Englishman... the mosque... Sultan Ahmed... obelisk... an Empire... the desert... Stravos Topouyoglou waiting for you... every day... noon... ooh!
Good God in heaven! Dead!
Farewell, Brindavoine...
AAA
BANG
YOU'LL NEVER MAKE IT TO ISTAN-BUL!
HA HA HA HA
ISTANBUL...

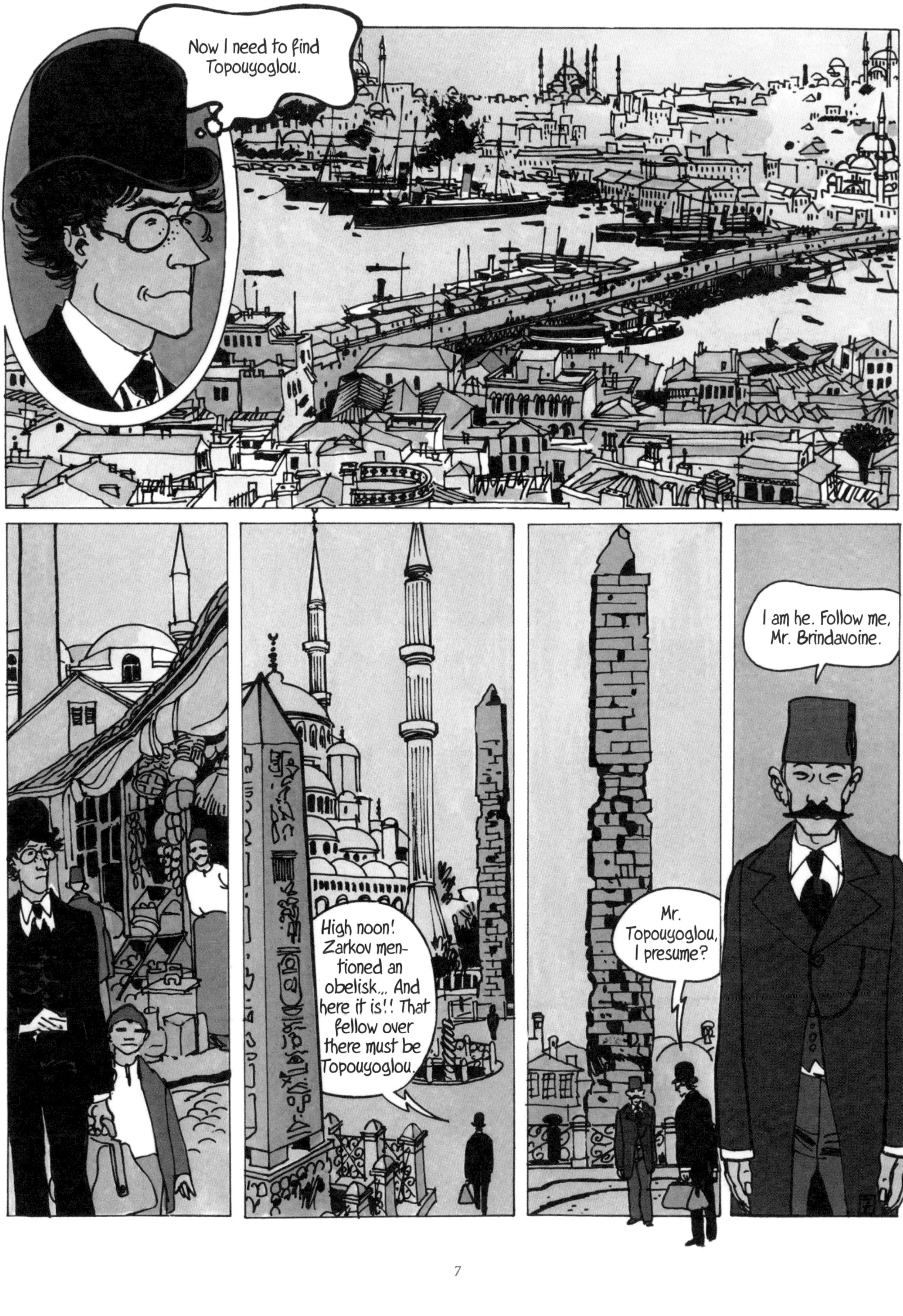
Now I need to find Topouyoglou.
High noon! Zarkov mentioned an obelisk... And here it is!! That fellow over there must be Topouyoglou.
Mr. Topouyoglou, I presume?
I am he. Follow me, Mr. Brindavoine.

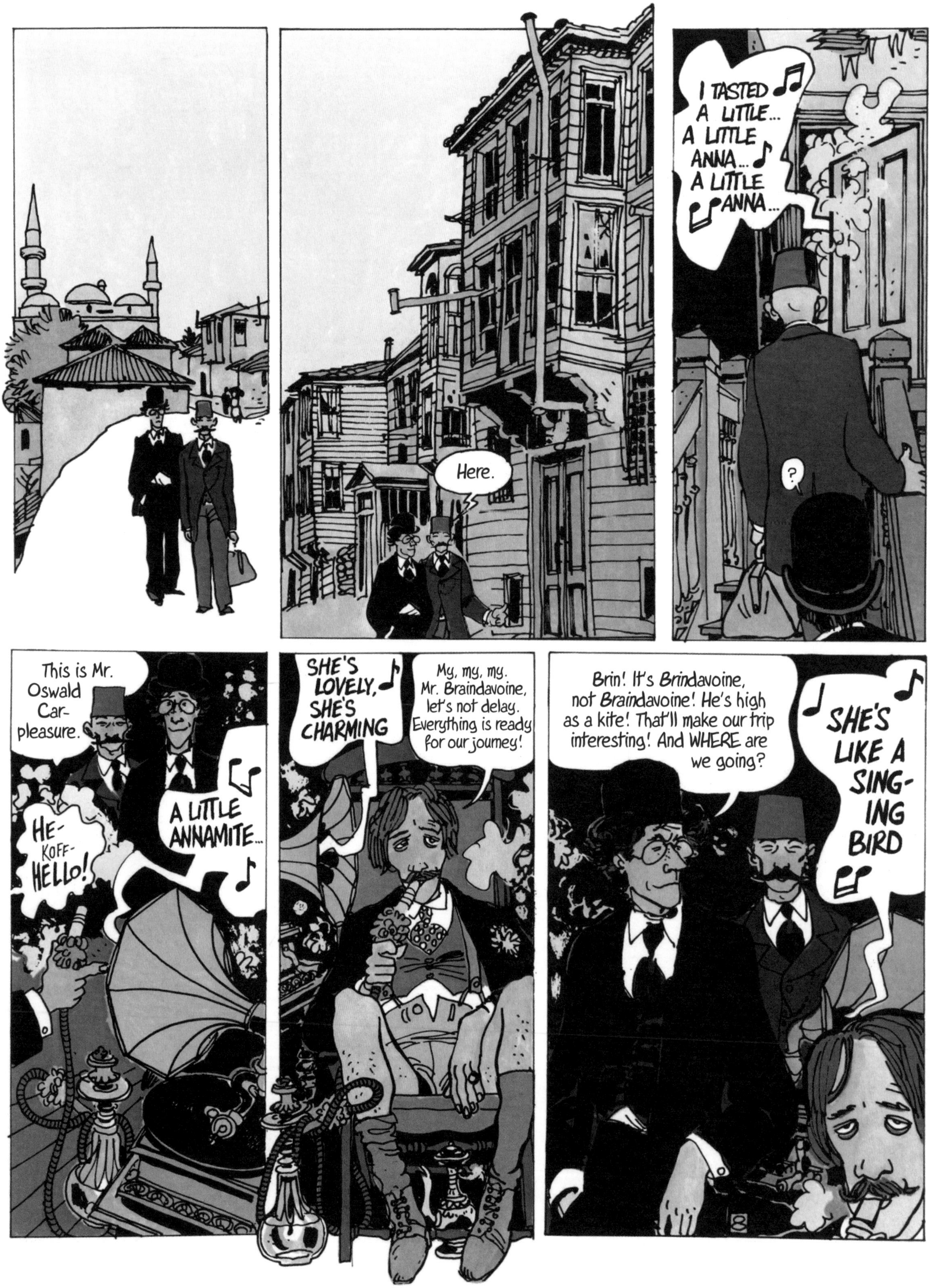
Here.
I TASTED A LITTLE... A LITTLE ANNA... A LITTLE ANNA...
?
This is Mr. Oswald Car-pleasure.
HE- KOFF- HELLO!
A LITTLE ANNAMITE...
SHE'S LOVELY, SHE'S CHARMING
My, my, my. Mr. Braindavoine, let's not delay. Everything is ready for our journey!
Brin! It's Brindavoine, not Braindavoine! He's high as a kite! That'll make our trip interesting! And WHERE are we going?
SHE'S LIKE A SING-ING BIRD

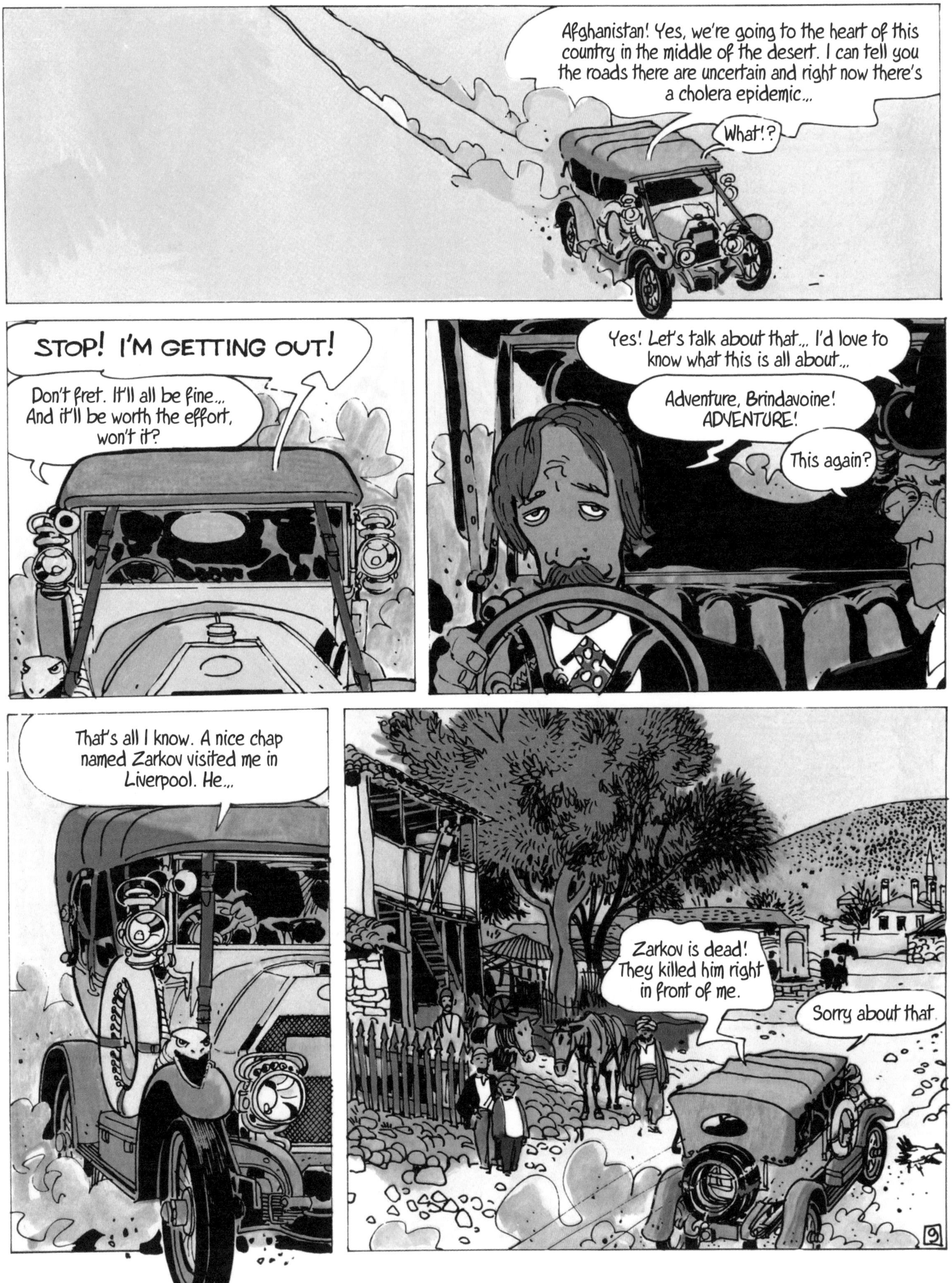
Afghanistan! Yes, we're going to the heart of this country in the middle of the desert. I can tell you the roads there are uncertain and right now there's a cholera epidemic...
What!?
STOP! I'M GETTING OUT!
Don't fret. It'll all be fine... And it'll be worth the effort, won't it?
Yes! Let's talk about that... I'd love to know what this is all about...
Adventure, Brindavoine! ADVENTURE!
This again?
That's all I know. A nice chap named Zarkov visited me in Liverpool. He...
Zarkov is dead! They killed him right in front of me.
Sorry about that.
9

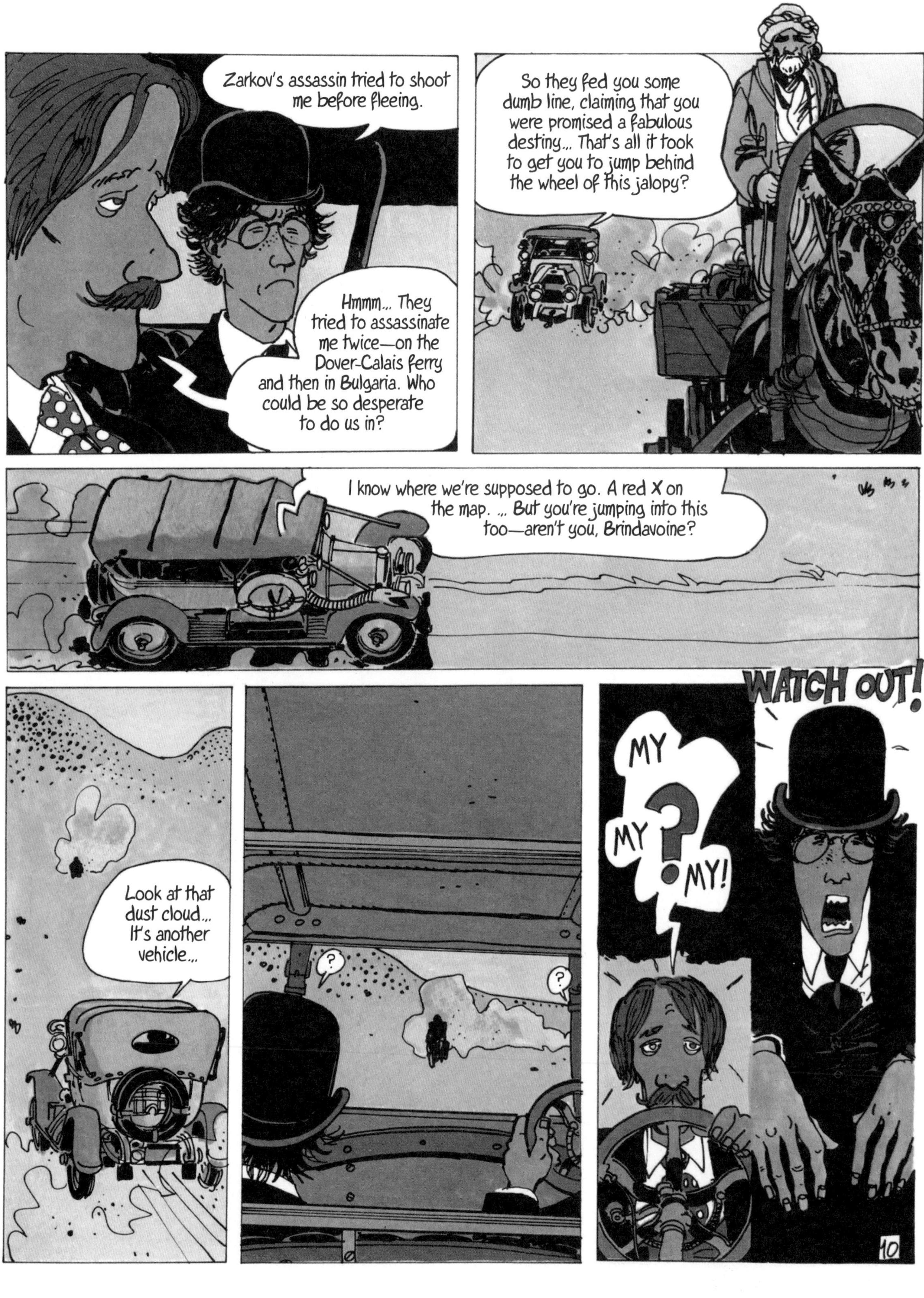
Zarkov's assassin tried to shoot me before fleeing.
Hmmm... They tried to assassinate me twice—on the Dover-Calais ferry and then in Bulgaria. Who could be so desperate to do us in?
So they fed you some dumb line, claiming that you were promised a fabulous destiny... That's all it took to get you to jump behind the wheel of this jalopy?
I know where we're supposed to go. A red X on the map. ... But you're jumping into this too—aren't you, Brindavoine?
Look at that dust cloud... It's another vehicle...
?
?
MY MY ? MY!
WATCH OUT!
10

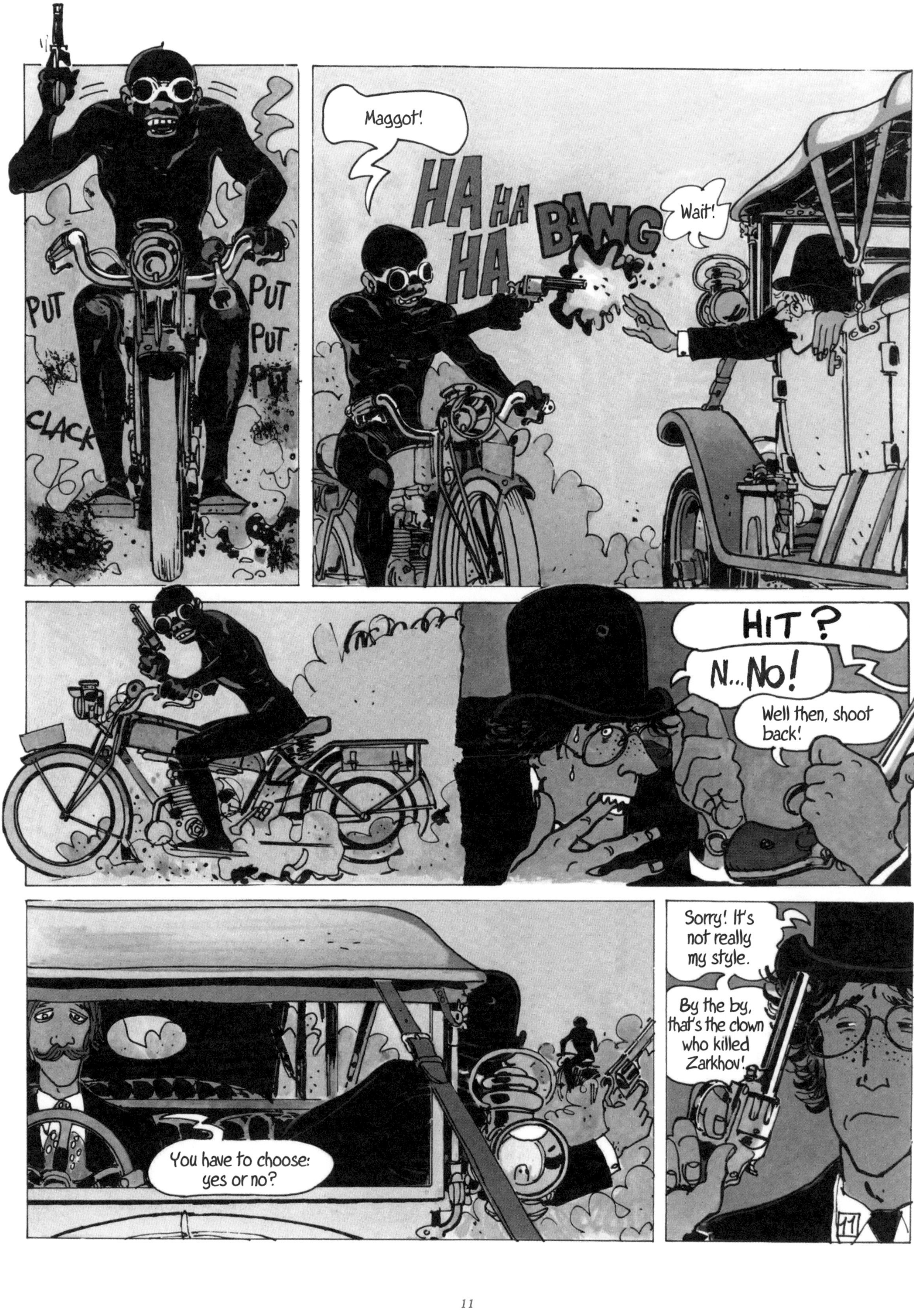
PUT
PUT
PUT
PUT
CLACK
Maggot!
HA HA HA HA
BANG
Wait!
HIT?
N...No!
Well then, shoot back!
You have to choose: yes or no?
Sorry! It's not really my style.
By the by, that's the clown who killed Zarkhov!
11

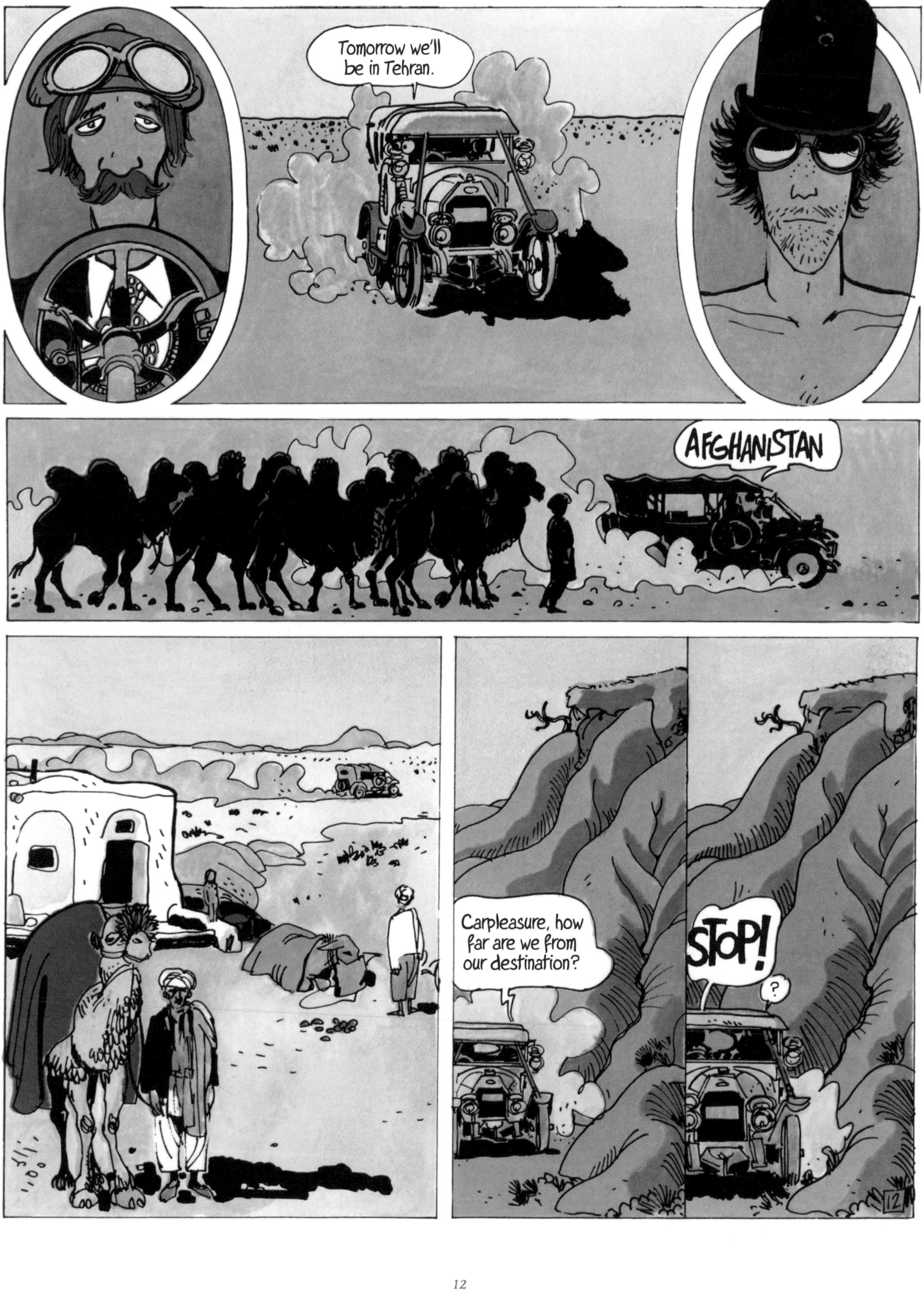

Tomorrow we'll be in Tehran.
AFGHANISTAN
Carpleasure, how far are we from our destination?
STOP!
?
12

Tea time!

Hey now, it sounded like this was urgent... This better be good.

You should have a cuppa.

MY TONKIN MY TONKIN MY TONKIN GIRL

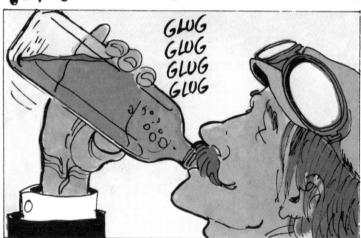

GLUG
GLUG
GLUG
GLUG

Whiskey, Lucien?

GLUG
GLUG
GLUG

GLUG
GLUG

GLUG

13

My... my... my...
Empty... No fear...
I have... plenty... 'n
my... suit...case...

Oswald... jus' b'tween you 'n' me...
That Tonkin girl... caught
yer... yer eye... uh...
I get... that... and
w-whiskey, I'm...
a big fan... but...
stoppin' that lemon
in full sun... fer
a... cuppa tea,
thass where
I...

It's my habit... ol' Lucien...
Five o'clock and hey pres-
to... I knock back a
glass or two... 'cause
you see... in Liverpool,
I was bored to tears.
Here, too... I thought
that this adven-
ture w-would
amuse... hurgh...
but no. And
now we have
to wipe the
smile off
our faces...

RRRRRRRR

?

HEY!
Carpleazurr,
look! Wh—wh—
what's that?

RRRRRR

An airplane!

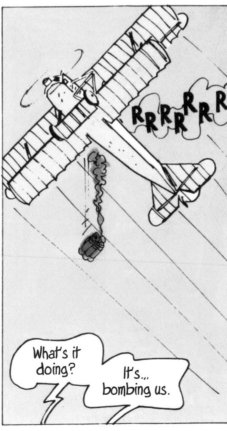

RRRRRRR

What's it
doing?

It's...
bombing us.

OH MY HO
HA HO
HA HA

HMPFFF

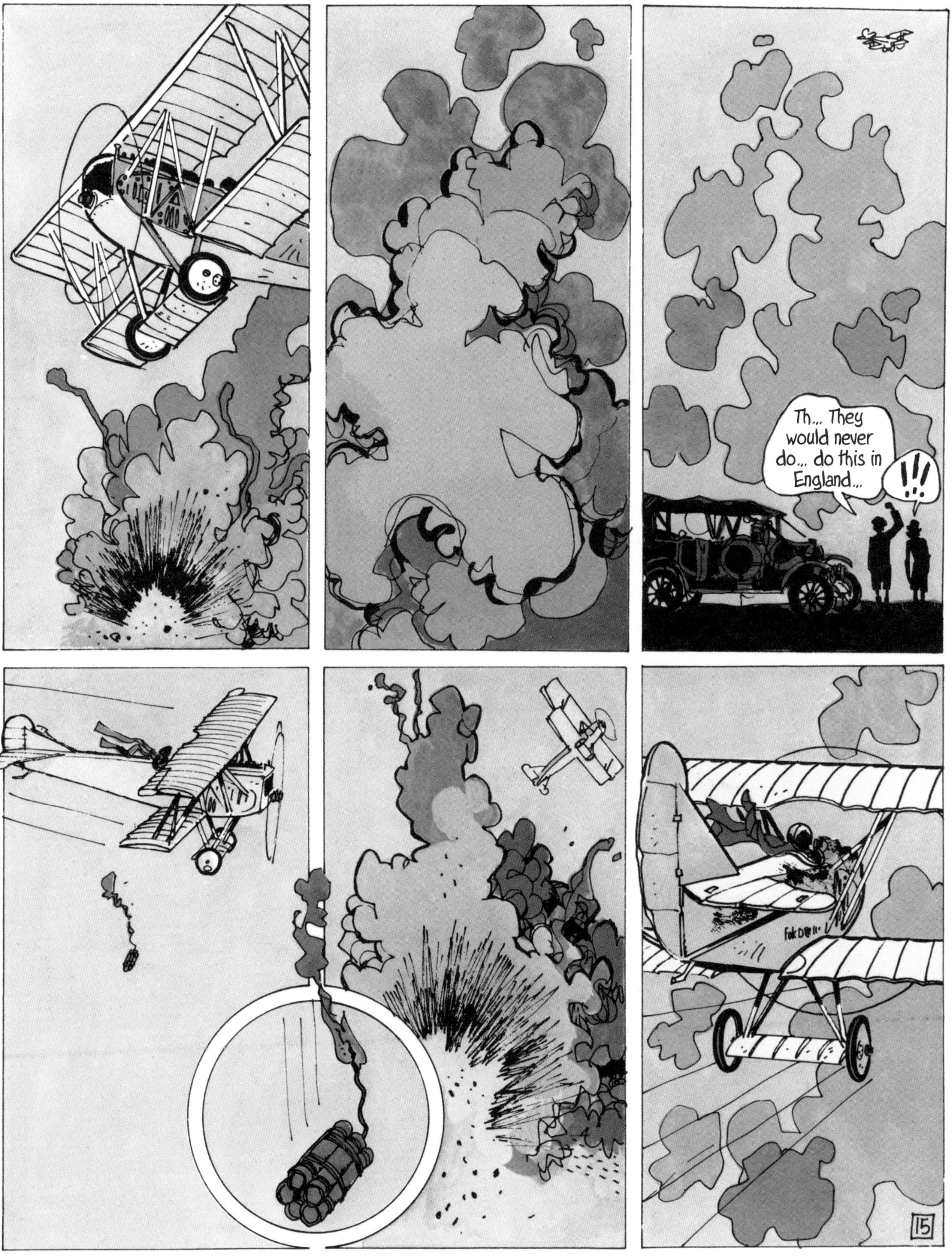
Th... They would never do... do this in England...
!!!
15

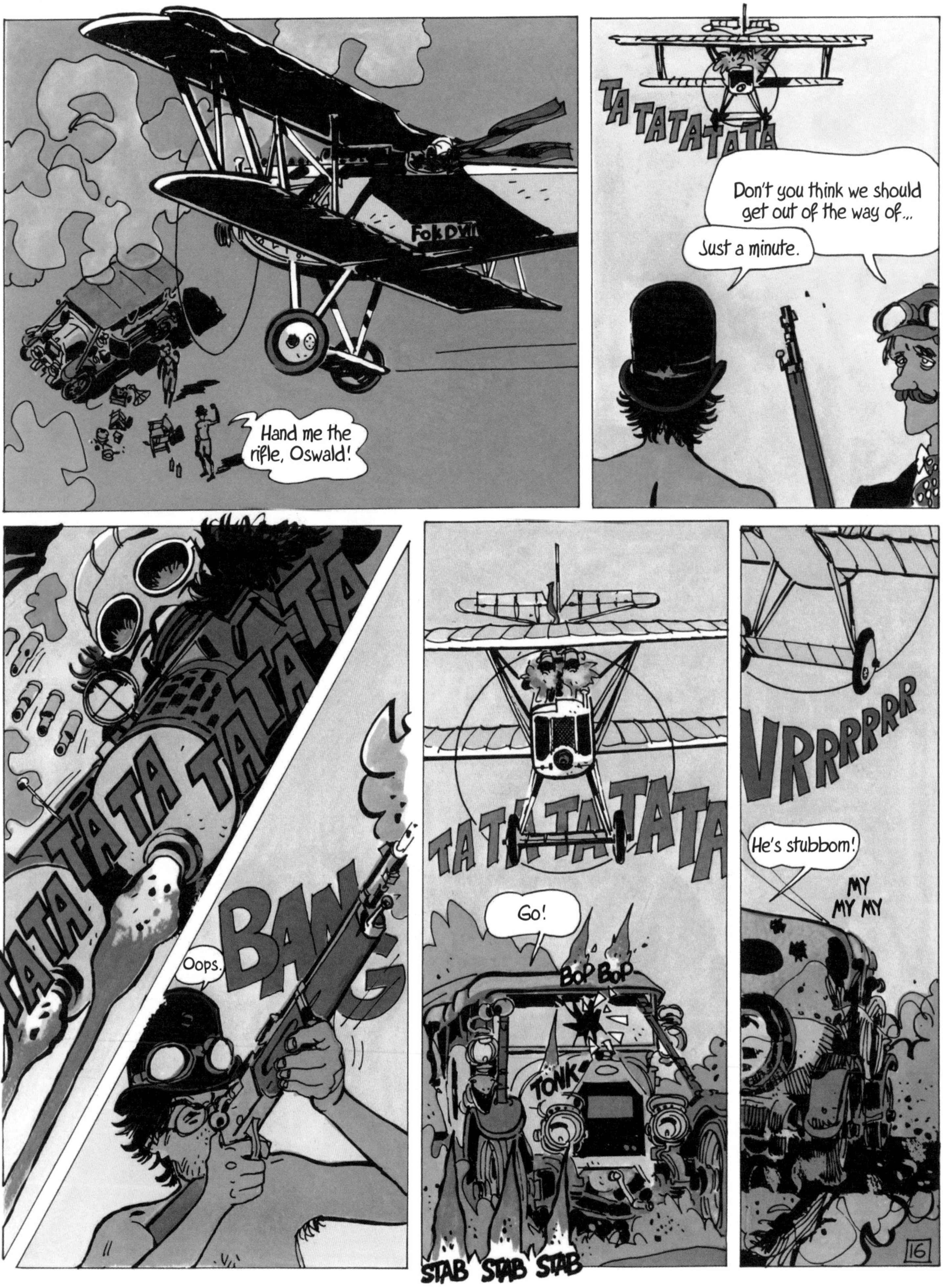
FokDVII
Hand me the rifle, Oswald!
TA TATATATATA
Don't you think we should get out of the way of...
Just a minute.
TATATATATATATA
BANG
Oops.
TATATATATATA
Go!
BOP BOP
TONK
STAB STAB STAB
VRRRRRR
He's stubborn!
MY MY MY
16

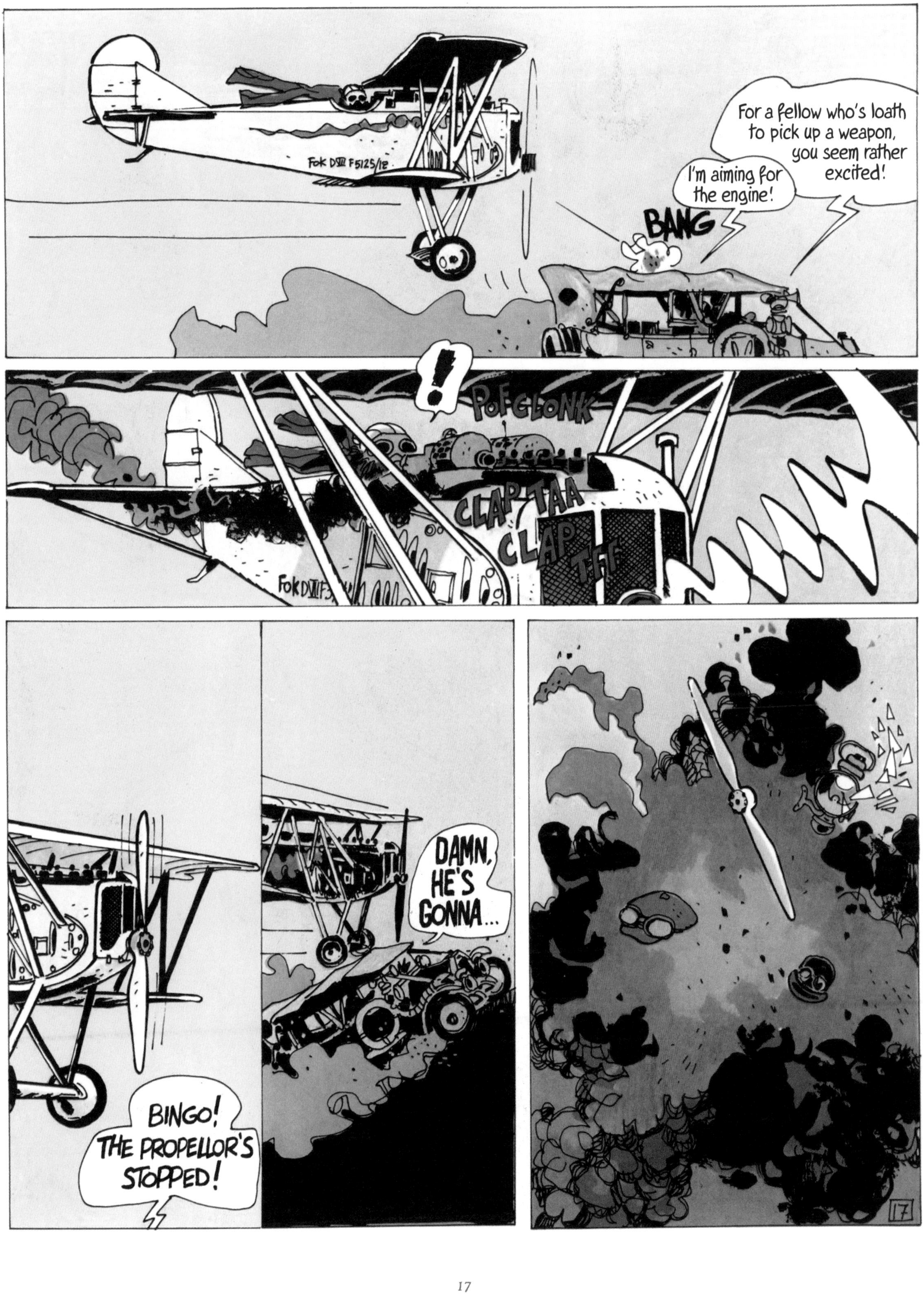

Fok DVII F5125/18
For a fellow who's loath to pick up a weapon, you seem rather excited!
I'm aiming for the engine!
BANG
!
POF CLONK
CLAP TAA
CLAP TFF
Fok DVII F5
DAMN, HE'S GONNA...
BINGO! THE PROPELLOR'S STOPPED!
17

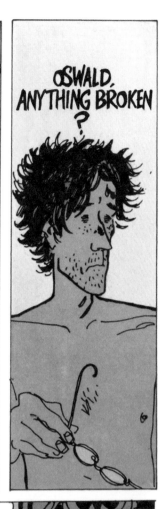
OSWALD, ANYTHING BROKEN?

Look at the pilot.

I'm glad to see he looks roughed up.

GOOD GOD! OSWALD, COME SEE!

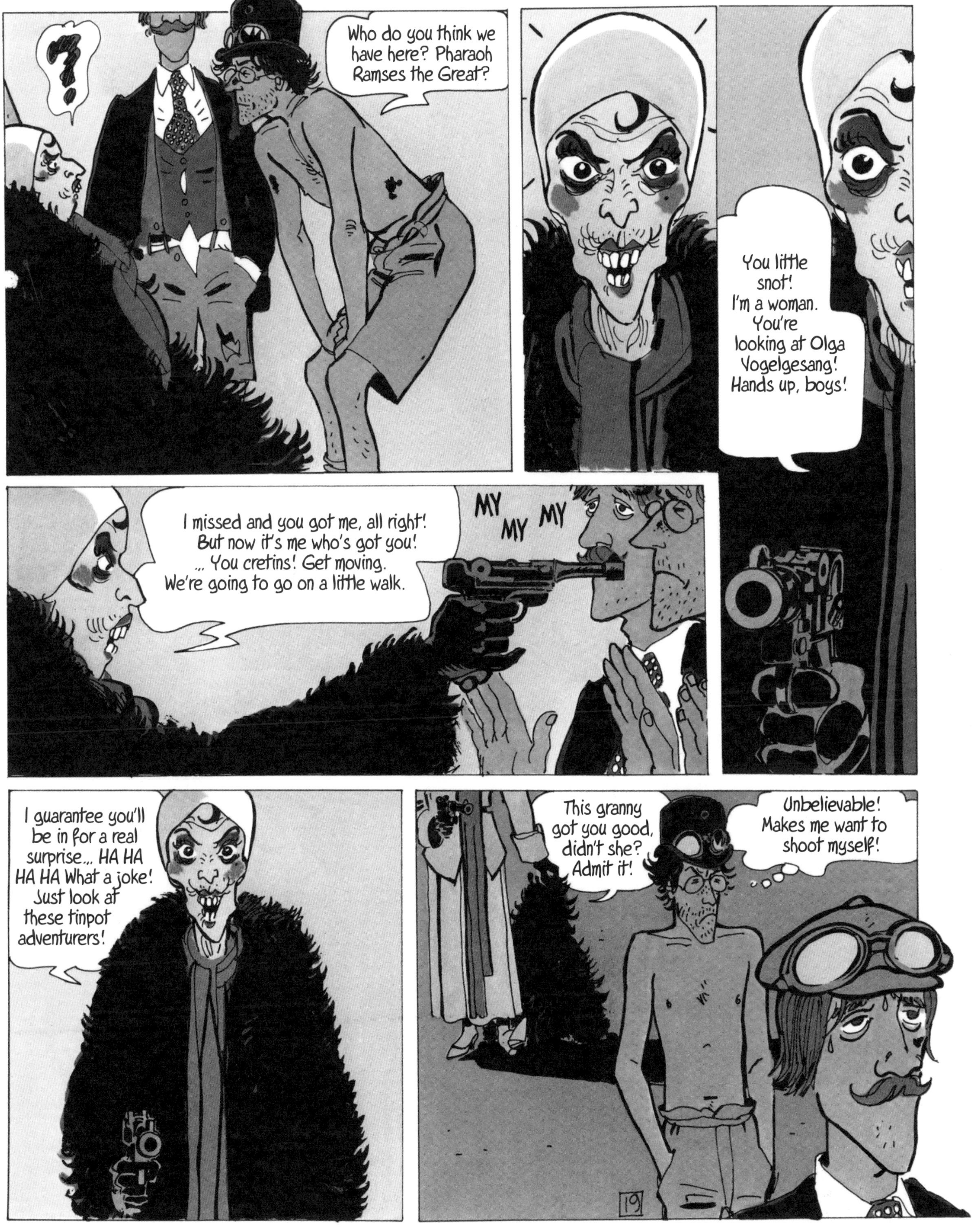
?
Who do you think we have here? Pharaoh Ramses the Great?
You little snot! I'm a woman. You're looking at Olga Vogelgesang! Hands up, boys!
I missed and you got me, all right! But now it's me who's got you! ... You cretins! Get moving. We're going to go on a little walk.
MY MY MY
I guarantee you'll be in for a real surprise... HA HA HA HA What a joke! Just look at these tinpot adventurers!
This granny got you good, didn't she? Admit it!
Unbelievable! Makes me want to shoot myself!
19

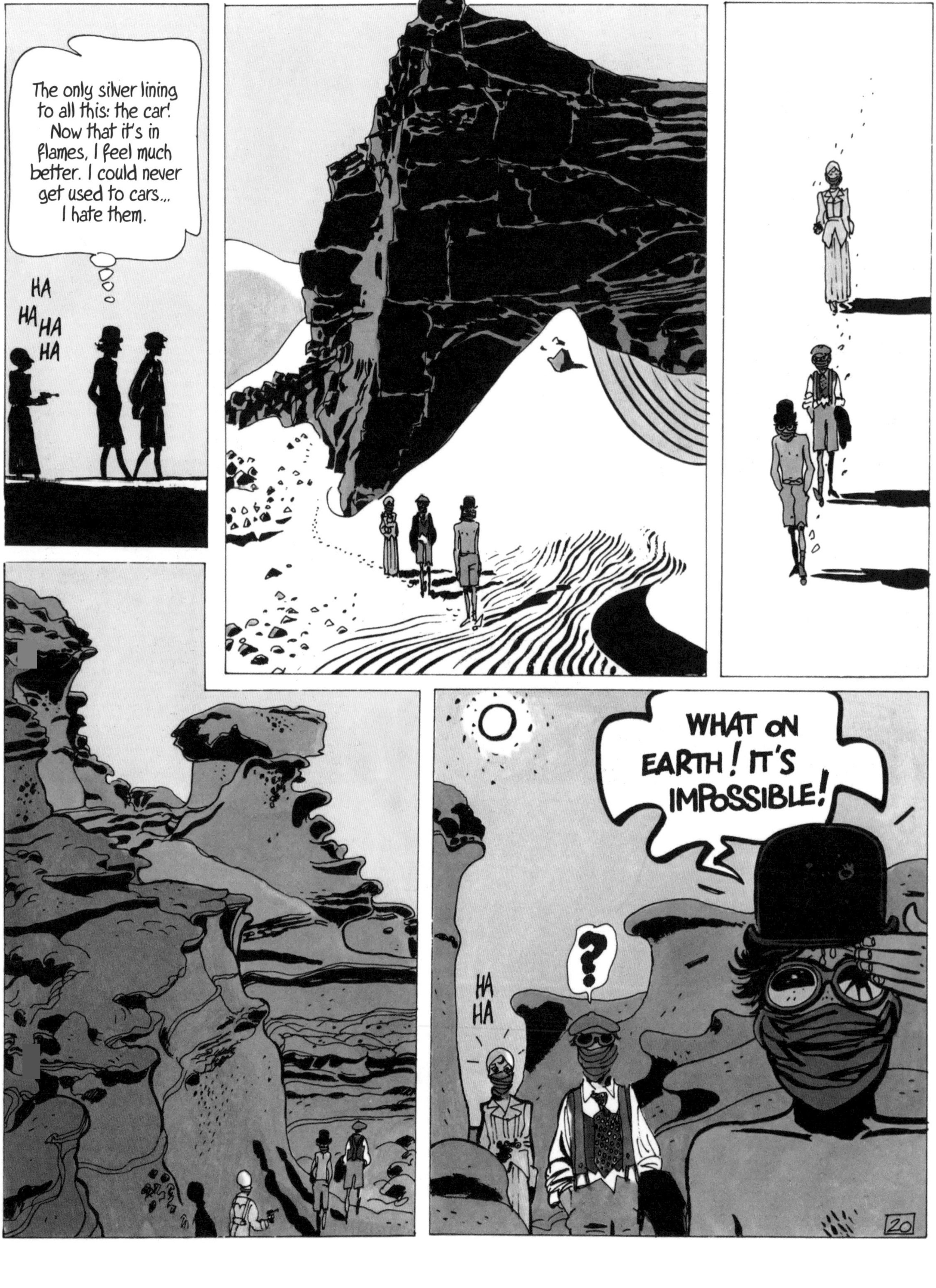
The only silver lining to all this: the car! Now that it's in flames, I feel much better. I could never get used to cars... I hate them.
HA HA HA HA
WHAT ON EARTH! IT'S IMPOSSIBLE!
?
HA HA

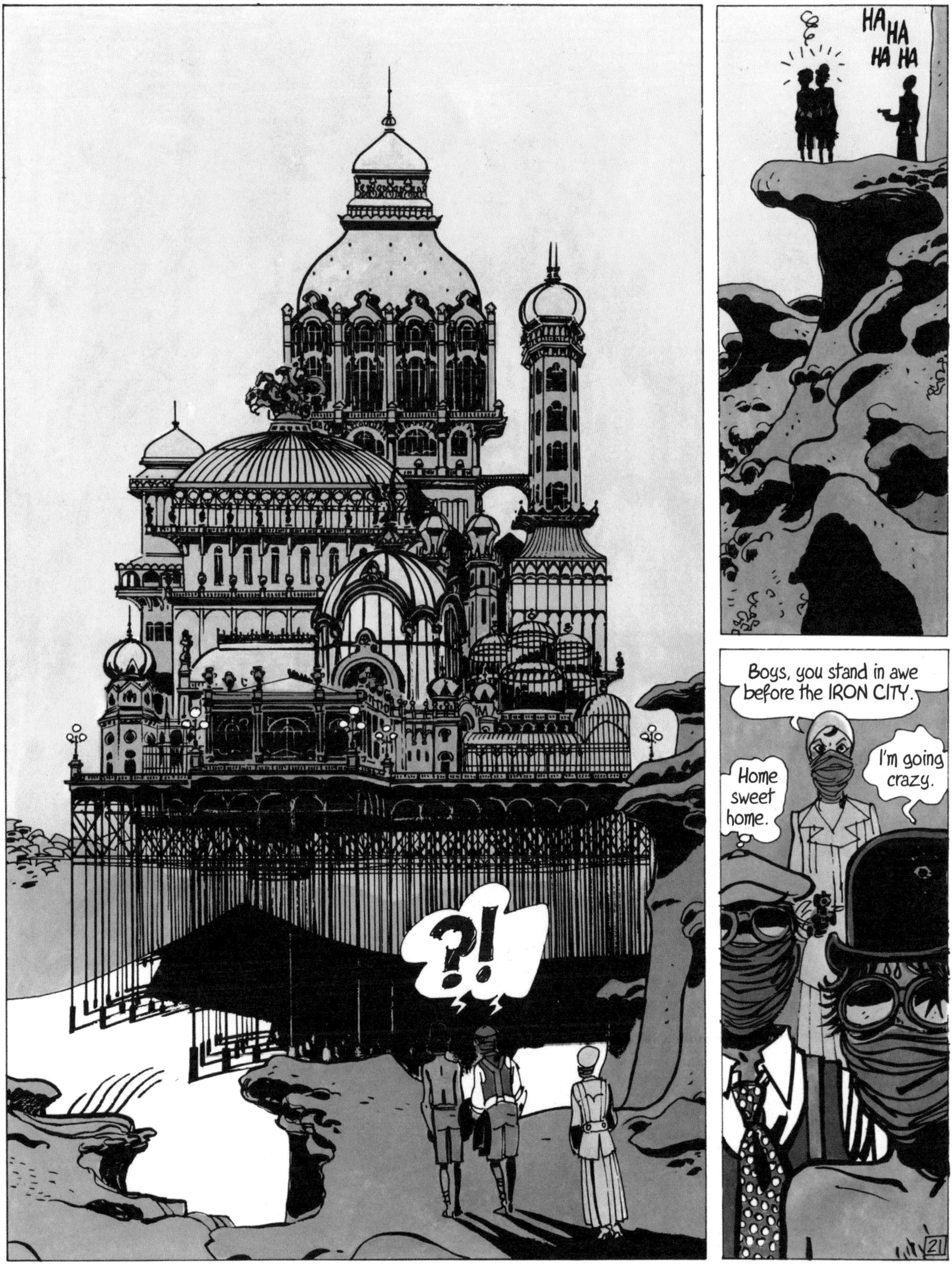
?!
HA HA HA HA
Boys, you stand in awe before the IRON CITY.
Home sweet home.
I'm going crazy.
21

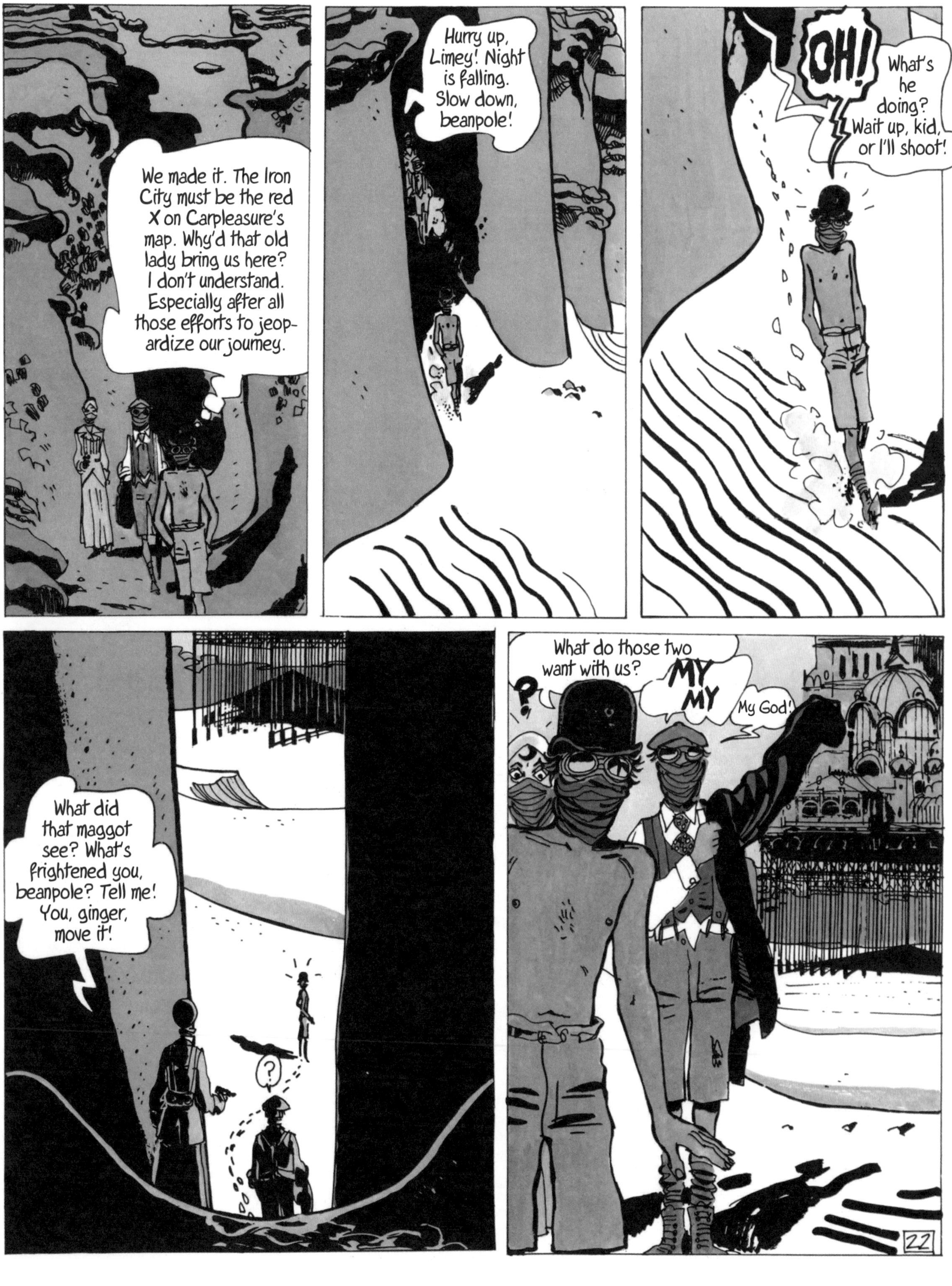

We made it. The Iron City must be the red X on Carpleasure's map. Why'd that old lady bring us here? I don't understand. Especially after all those efforts to jeopardize our journey.
Hurry up, Limey! Night is falling. Slow down, beanpole!
OH!
What's he doing? Wait up, kid, or I'll shoot!
What did that maggot see? What's frightened you, beanpole? Tell me! You, ginger, move it!
?
What do those two want with us?
?
MY MY
My God!
22

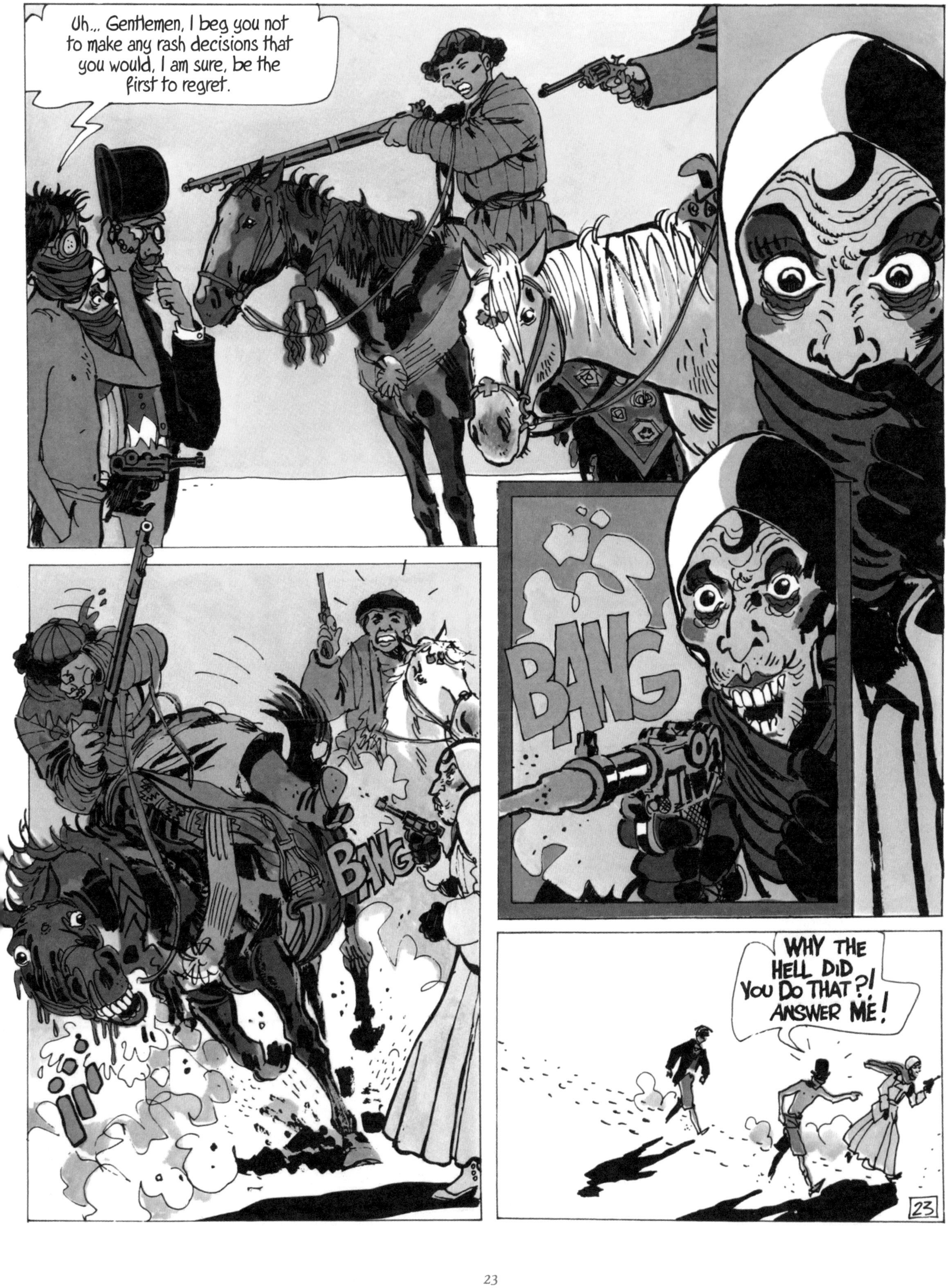
Uh... Gentlemen, I beg you not to make any rash decisions that you would, I am sure, be the first to regret.
BANG
BANG
WHY THE HELL DID YOU DO THAT?! ANSWER ME!
23

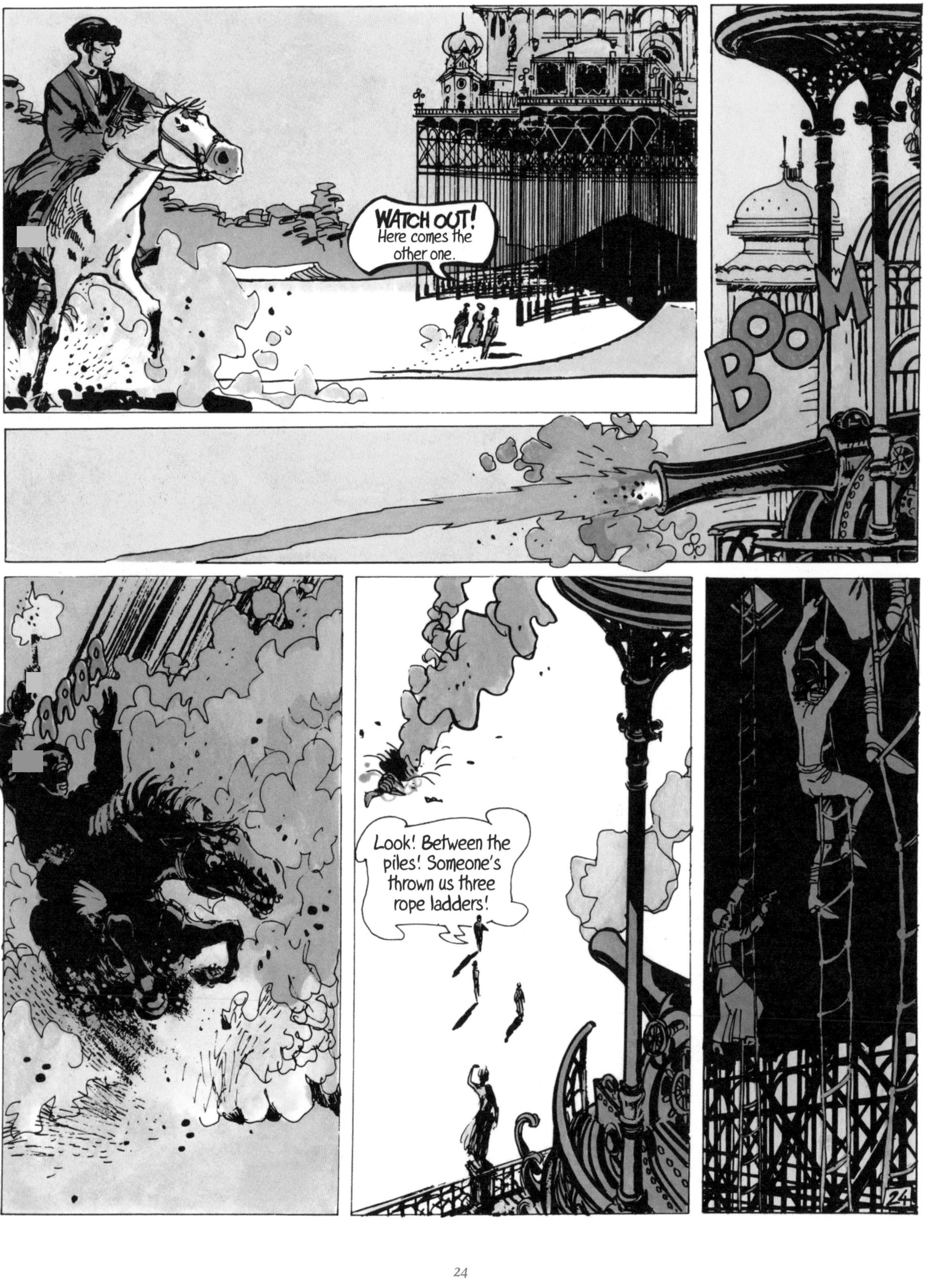
WATCH OUT! Here comes the other one.
BOOM
Look! Between the piles! Someone's thrown us three rope ladders!

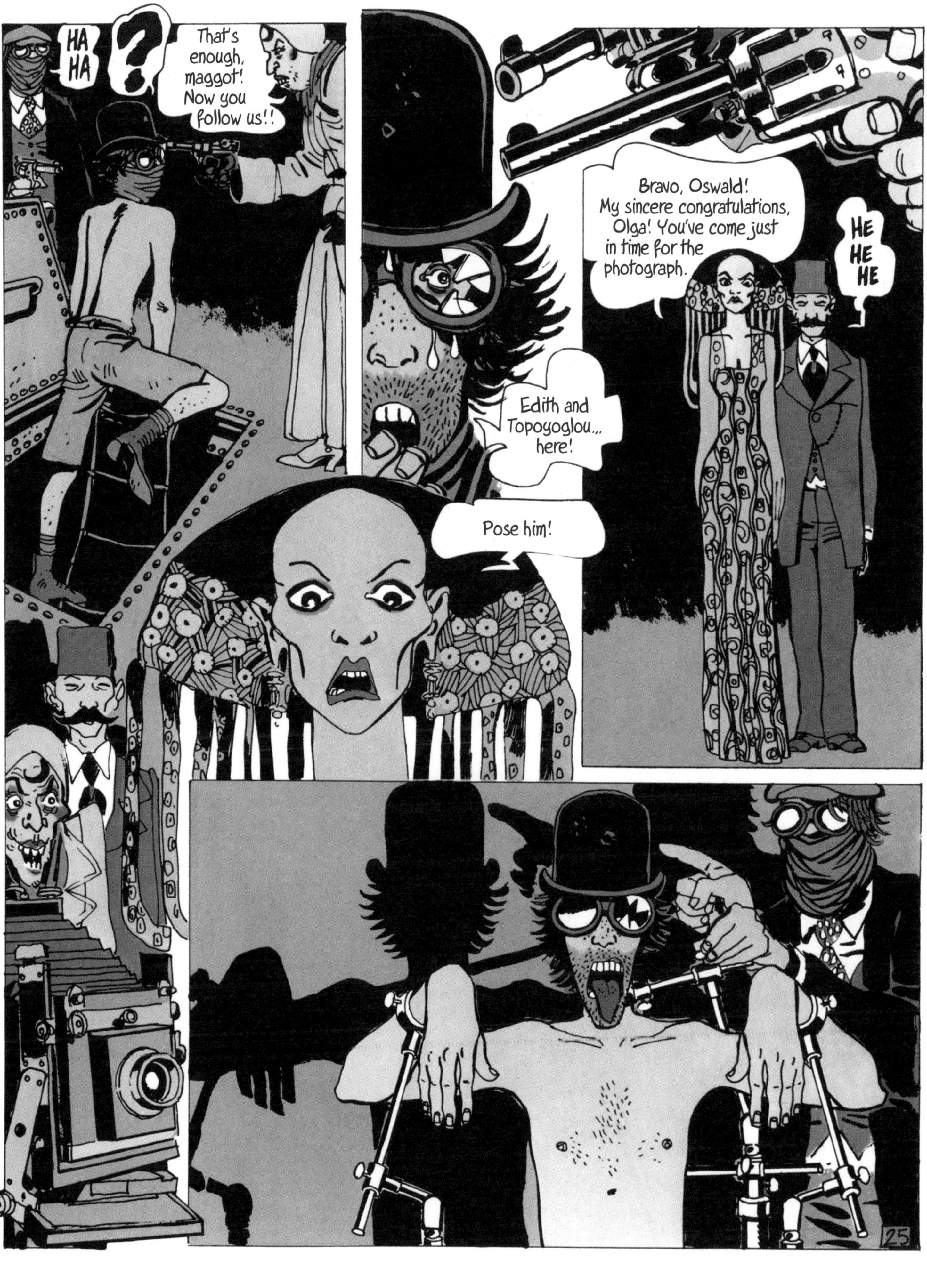
HA HA
?
That's enough, maggot! Now you follow us!!
Edith and Topoyoglou... here!
Bravo, Oswald! My sincere congratulations, Olga! You've come just in time for the photograph.
HE HE HE
Pose him!
25

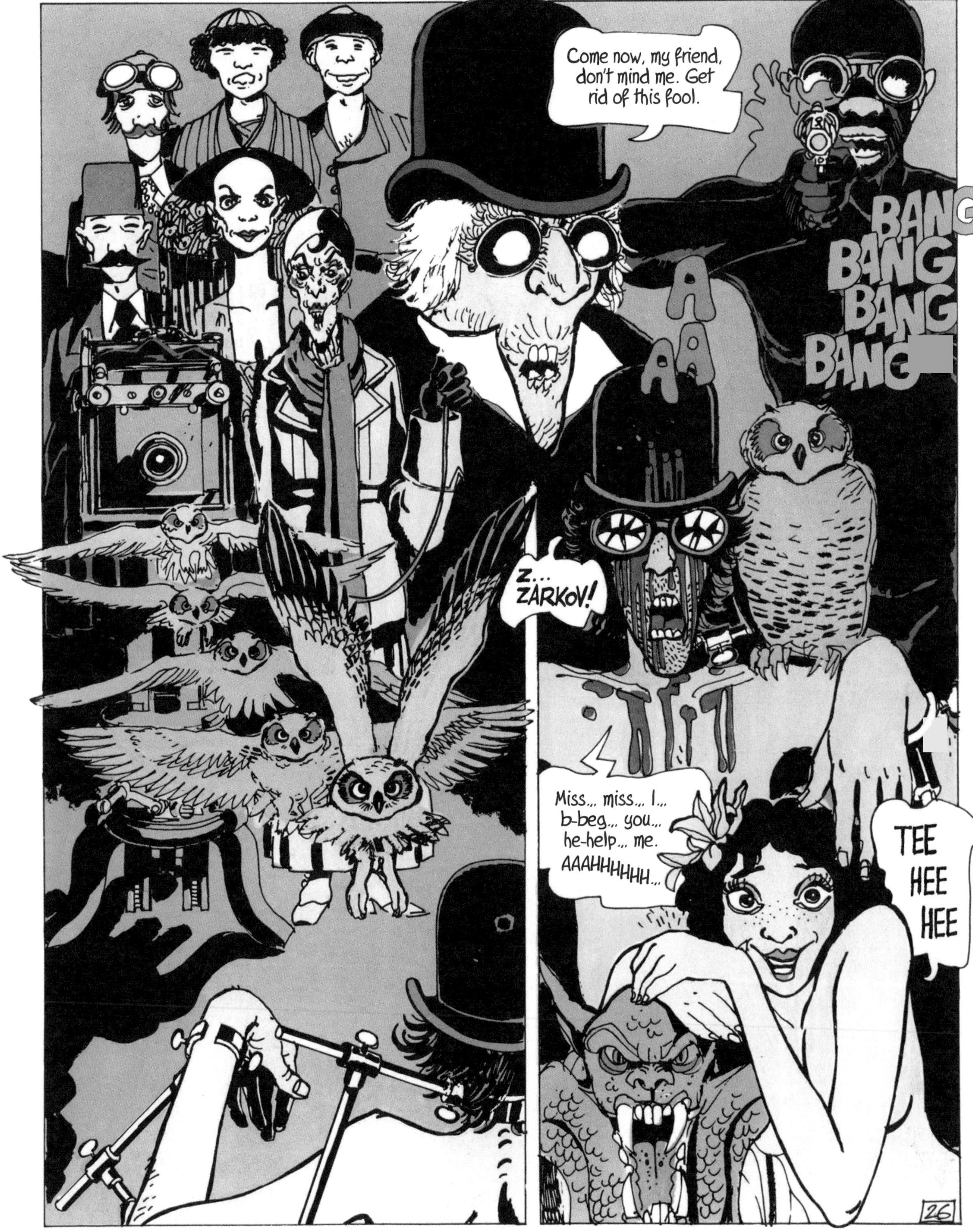
Come now, my friend, don't mind me. Get rid of this fool.
BANG BANG BANG BANG
A A A
Z... ZARKOV!
Miss... miss... I... b-beg... you... he-help... me. AAAHHHHHH...
TEE HEE HEE

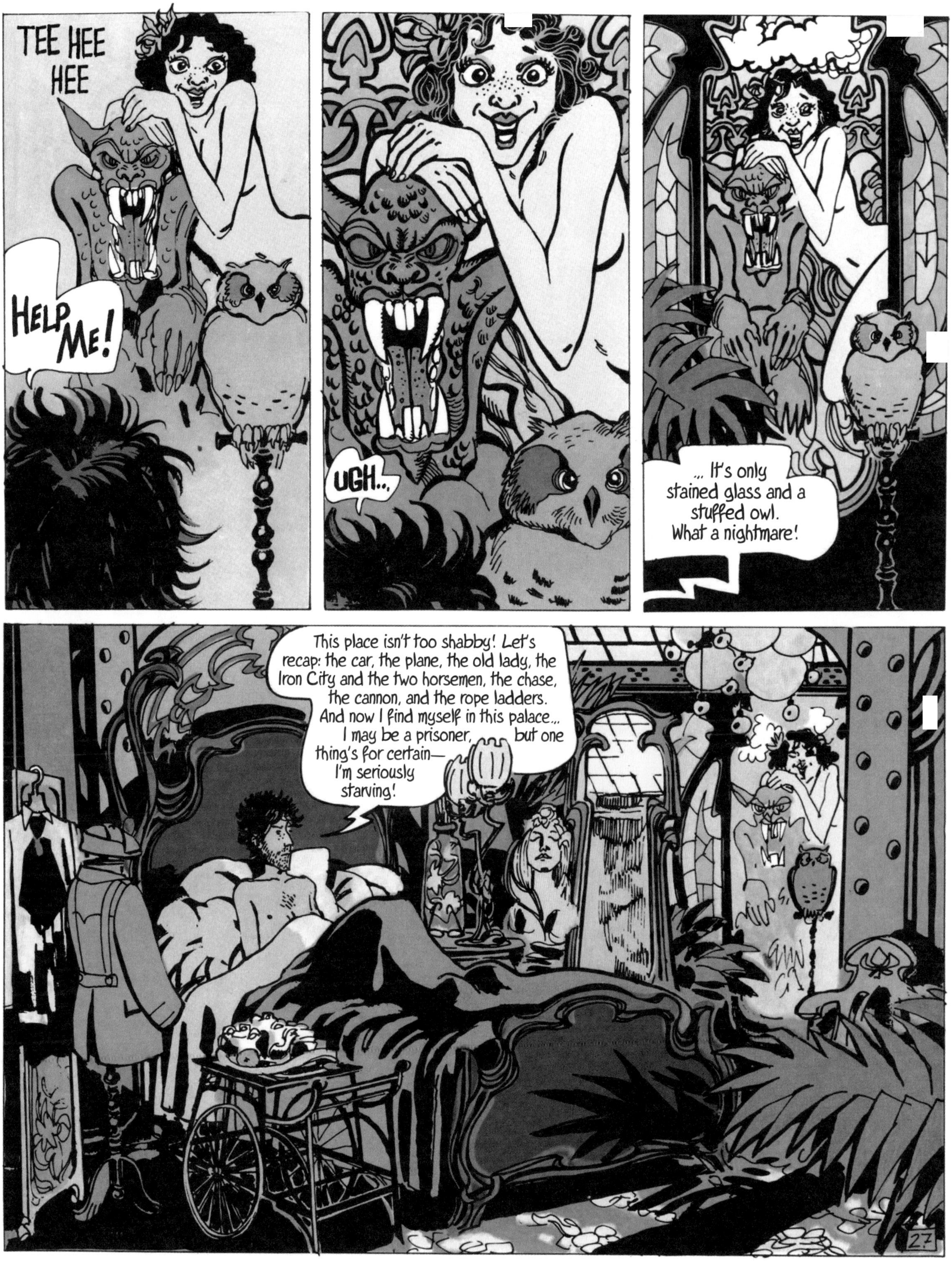
TEE HEE HEE
HELP ME!
UGH...
... It's only stained glass and a stuffed owl. What a nightmare!
This place isn't too shabby! Let's recap: the car, the plane, the old lady, the Iron City and the two horsemen, the chase, the cannon, and the rope ladders. And now I find myself in this palace... I may be a prisoner, but one thing's for certain— I'm seriously starving!

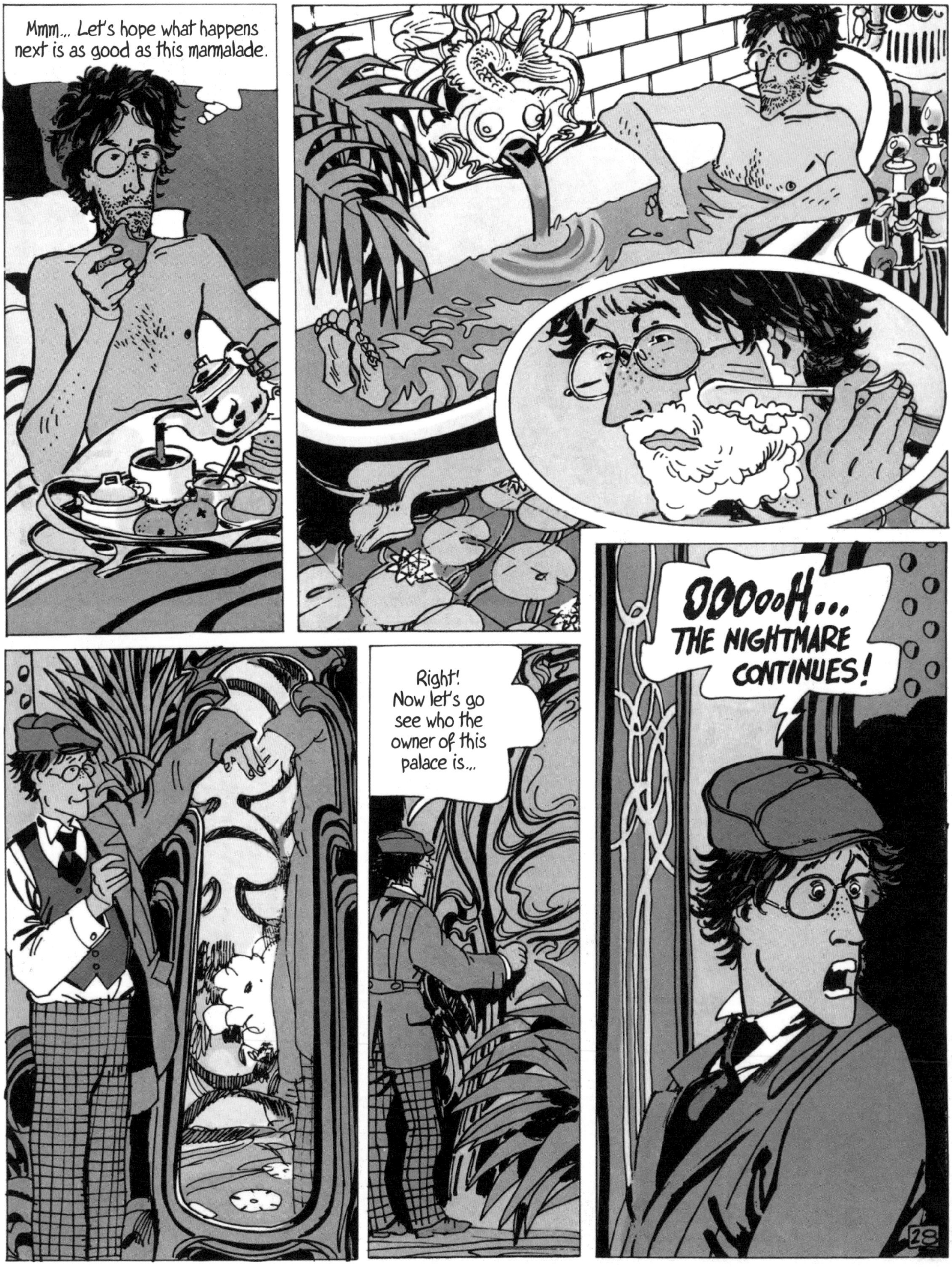
Mmm... Let's hope what happens next is as good as this marmalade.
OOOooH... THE NIGHTMARE CONTINUES!
Right! Now let's go see who the owner of this palace is...
28

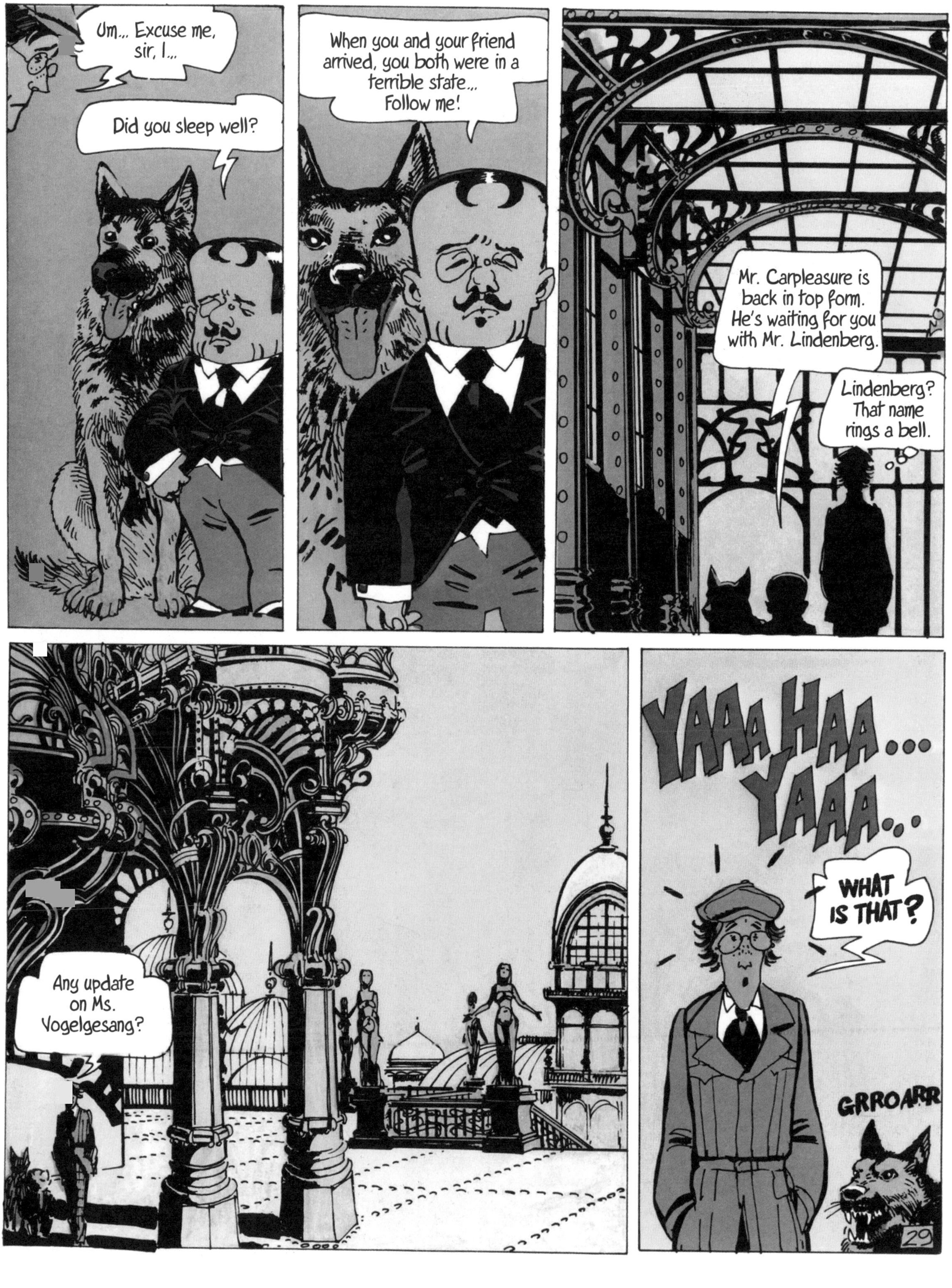
Um... Excuse me, sir, I...
Did you sleep well?
When you and your friend arrived, you both were in a terrible state... Follow me!
Mr. Carpleasure is back in top form. He's waiting for you with Mr. Lindenberg.
Lindenberg? That name rings a bell.
Any update on Ms. Vogelgesang?
YAAA HAA... YAAA...
WHAT IS THAT?
GRROARR
29

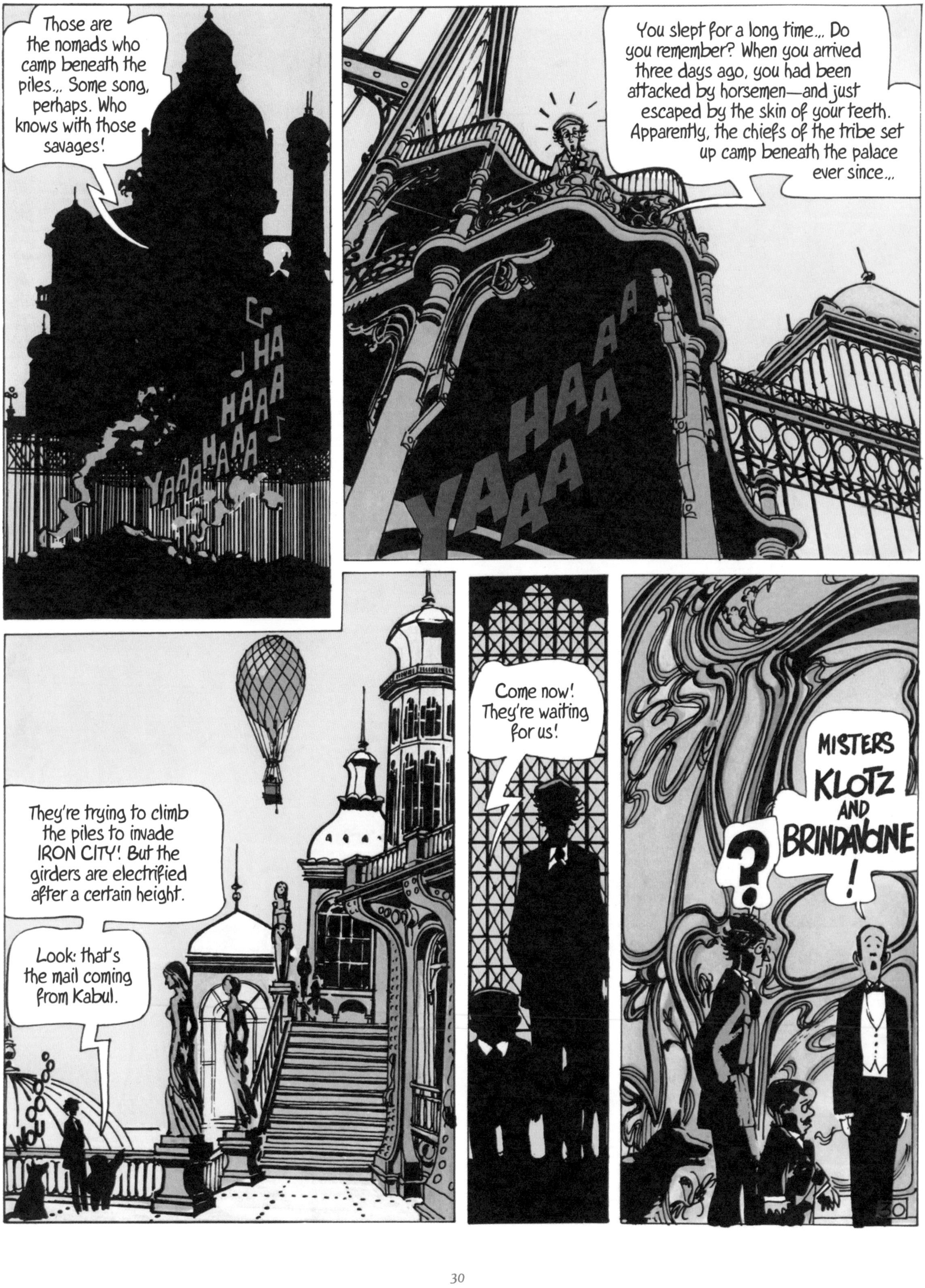

Those are the nomads who camp beneath the piles... Some song, perhaps. Who knows with those savages!
YAAAHAAAHAAAHA
You slept for a long time... Do you remember? When you arrived three days ago, you had been attacked by horsemen—and just escaped by the skin of your teeth. Apparently, the chiefs of the tribe set up camp beneath the palace ever since...
YAAAHAAAA
They're trying to climb the piles to invade IRON CITY! But the girders are electrified after a certain height.
Look: that's the mail coming from Kabul.
Come now! They're waiting for us!
MISTERS KLOTZ AND BRINDAVOINE !
?
30

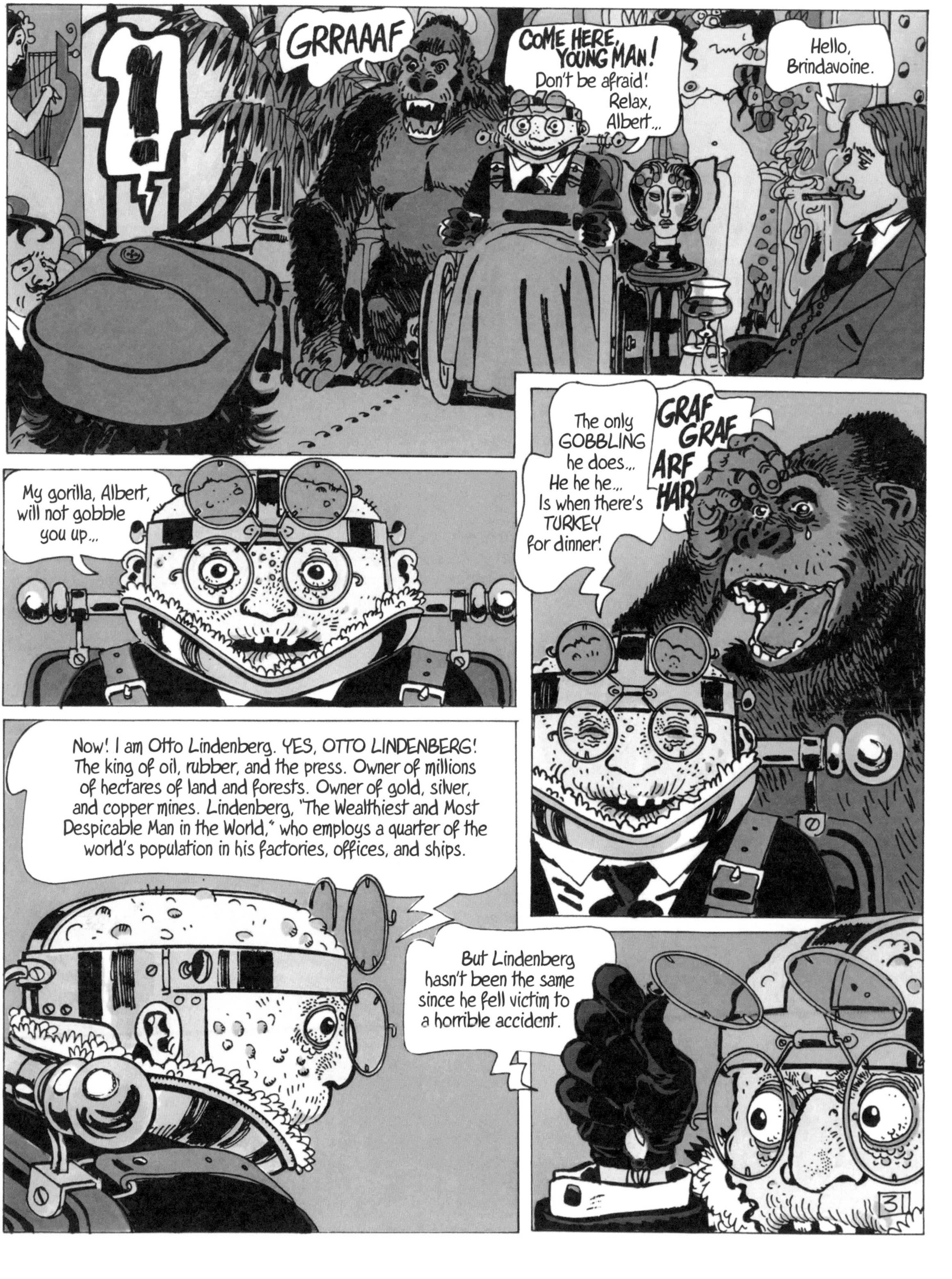
GRRAAAF
COME HERE, YOUNG MAN! Don't be afraid! Relax, Albert...
Hello, Brindavoine.
My gorilla, Albert, will not gobble you up...
The only GOBBLING he does... He he he... Is when there's TURKEY for dinner!
GRAF GRAF ARF HAR
Now! I am Otto Lindenberg. YES, OTTO LINDENBERG! The king of oil, rubber, and the press. Owner of millions of hectares of land and forests. Owner of gold, silver, and copper mines. Lindenberg, "The Wealthiest and Most Despicable Man in the World," who employs a quarter of the world's population in his factories, offices, and ships.
But Lindenberg hasn't been the same since he fell victim to a horrible accident.
31

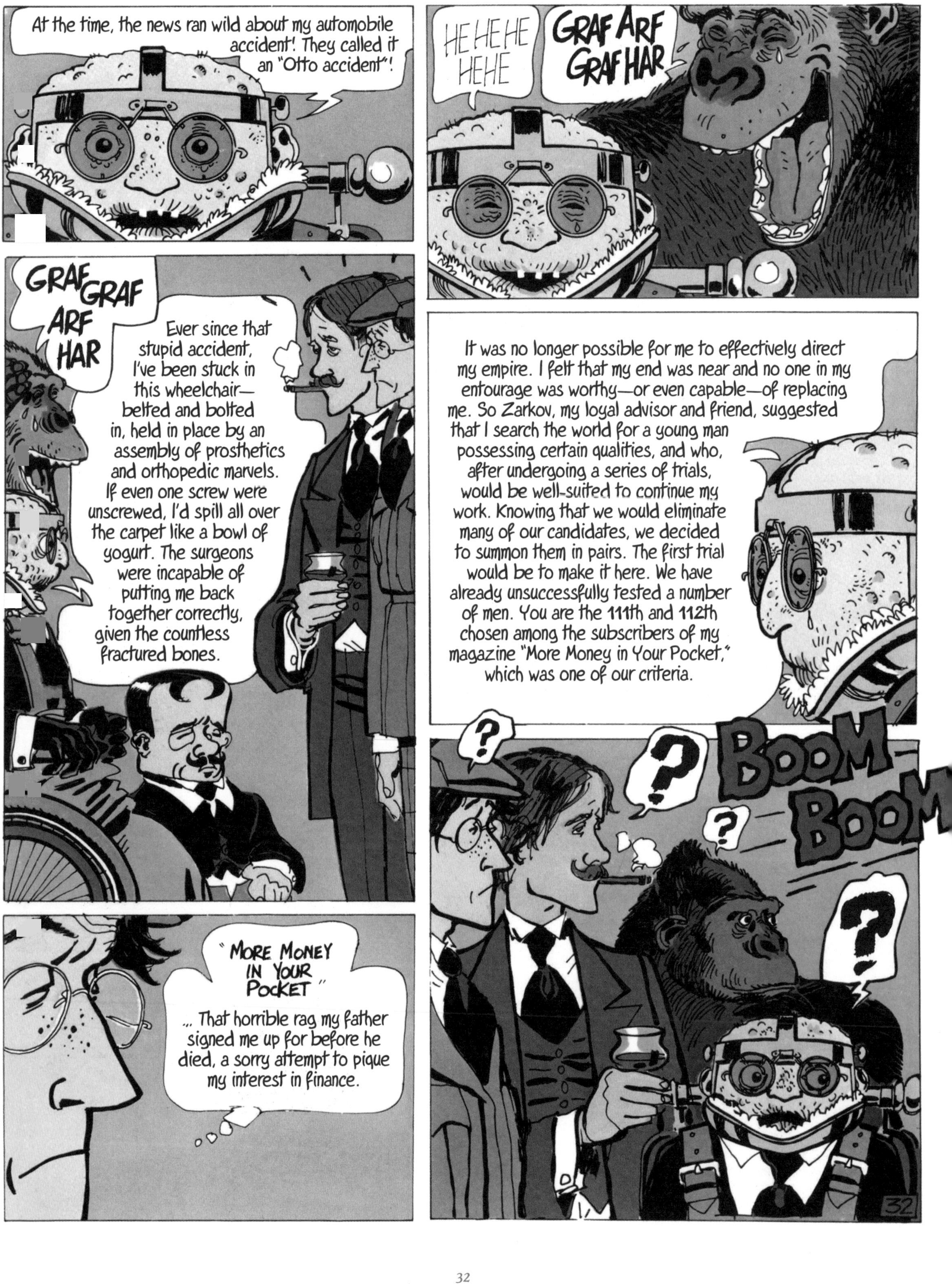

At the time, the news ran wild about my automobile accident! They called it an "Otto accident"!
HE HE HE HE HE
GRAF ARF GRAF HAR
GRAF GRAF ARF HAR
Ever since that stupid accident, I've been stuck in this wheelchair—belted and bolted in, held in place by an assembly of prosthetics and orthopedic marvels. If even one screw were unscrewed, I'd spill all over the carpet like a bowl of yogurt. The surgeons were incapable of putting me back together correctly, given the countless fractured bones.
It was no longer possible for me to effectively direct my empire. I felt that my end was near and no one in my entourage was worthy—or even capable—of replacing me. So Zarkov, my loyal advisor and friend, suggested that I search the world for a young man possessing certain qualities, and who, after undergoing a series of trials, would be well-suited to continue my work. Knowing that we would eliminate many of our candidates, we decided to summon them in pairs. The first trial would be to make it here. We have already unsuccessfully tested a number of men. You are the **111th** and **112th** chosen among the subscribers of my magazine "More Money in Your Pocket," which was one of our criteria.
"MORE MONEY IN YOUR POCKET"
... That horrible rag my father signed me up for before he died, a sorry attempt to pique my interest in finance.
?
?
?
?
BOOM-BOOM
32

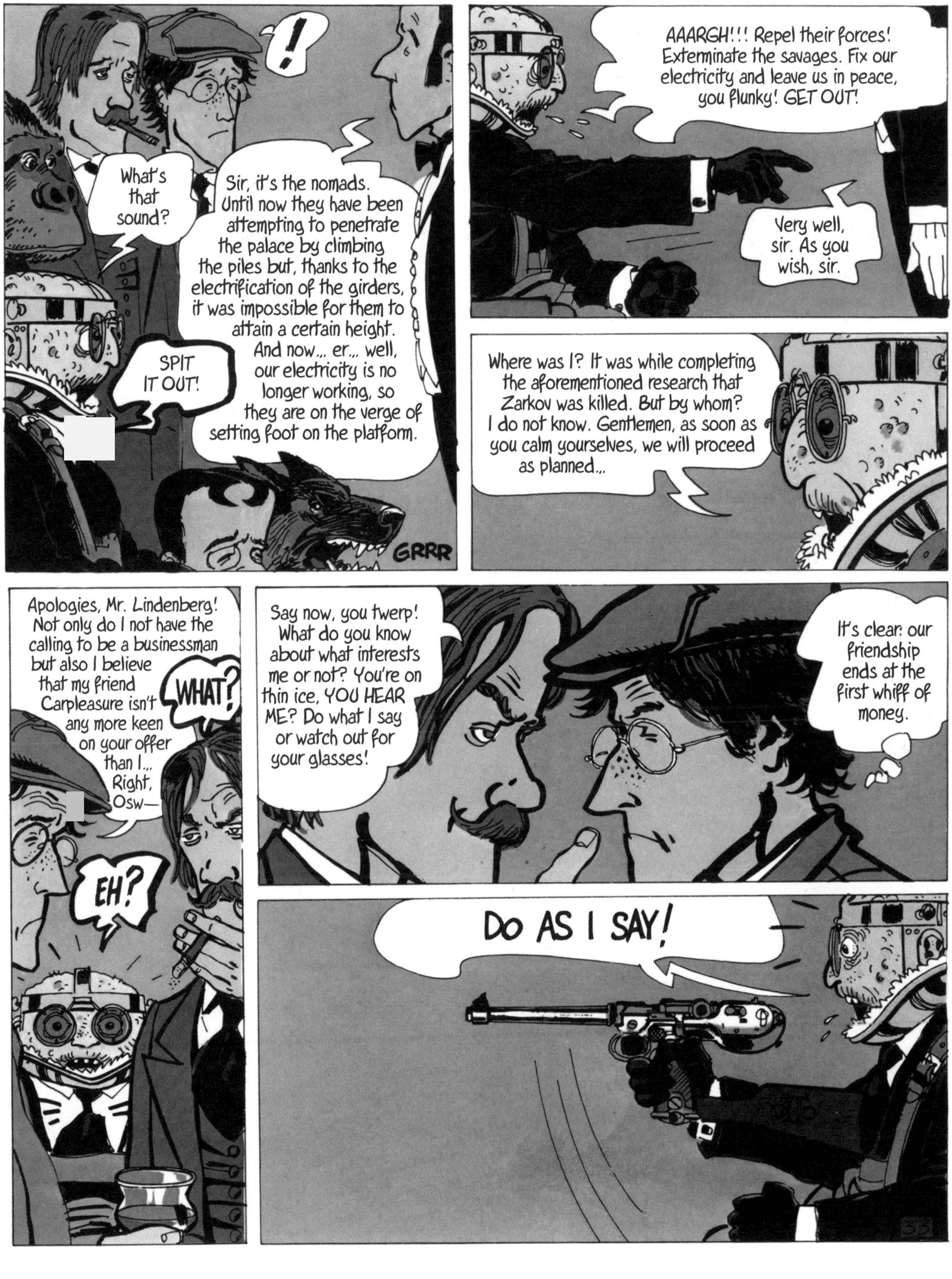

!
What's that sound?
Sir, it's the nomads. Until now they have been attempting to penetrate the palace by climbing the piles but, thanks to the electrification of the girders, it was impossible for them to attain a certain height. And now... er... well, our electricity is no longer working, so they are on the verge of setting foot on the platform.
SPIT IT OUT!
GRRR
AAARGH!!! Repel their forces! Exterminate the savages. Fix our electricity and leave us in peace, you flunky! GET OUT!
Very well, sir. As you wish, sir.
Where was I? It was while completing the aforementioned research that Zarkov was killed. But by whom? I do not know. Gentlemen, as soon as you calm yourselves, we will proceed as planned...
Apologies, Mr. Lindenberg! Not only do I not have the calling to be a businessman but also I believe that my friend Carpleasure isn't any more keen on your offer than I... Right, Osw—
WHAT?
EH?
Say now, you twerp! What do you know about what interests me or not? You're on thin ice, YOU HEAR ME? Do what I say or watch out for your glasses!
It's clear: our friendship ends at the first whiff of money.
DO AS I SAY!

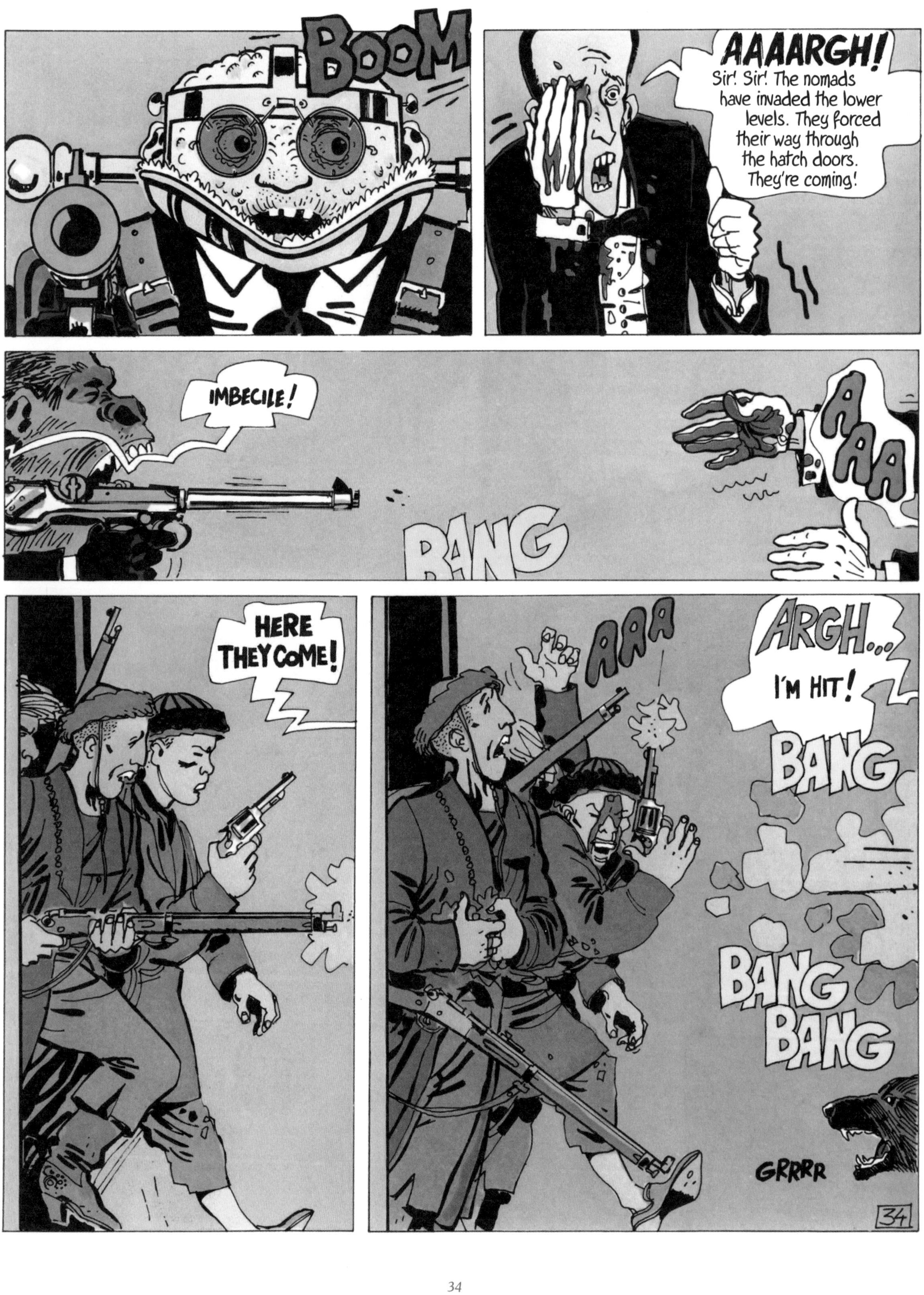
BOOM
AAAARGH!
Sir! Sir! The nomads have invaded the lower levels. They forced their way through the hatch doors. They're coming!
IMBECILE!
AAA
BANG
HERE THEY COME!
AAA
ARGH...
I'M HIT!
BANG
BANG BANG
GRRRR
34

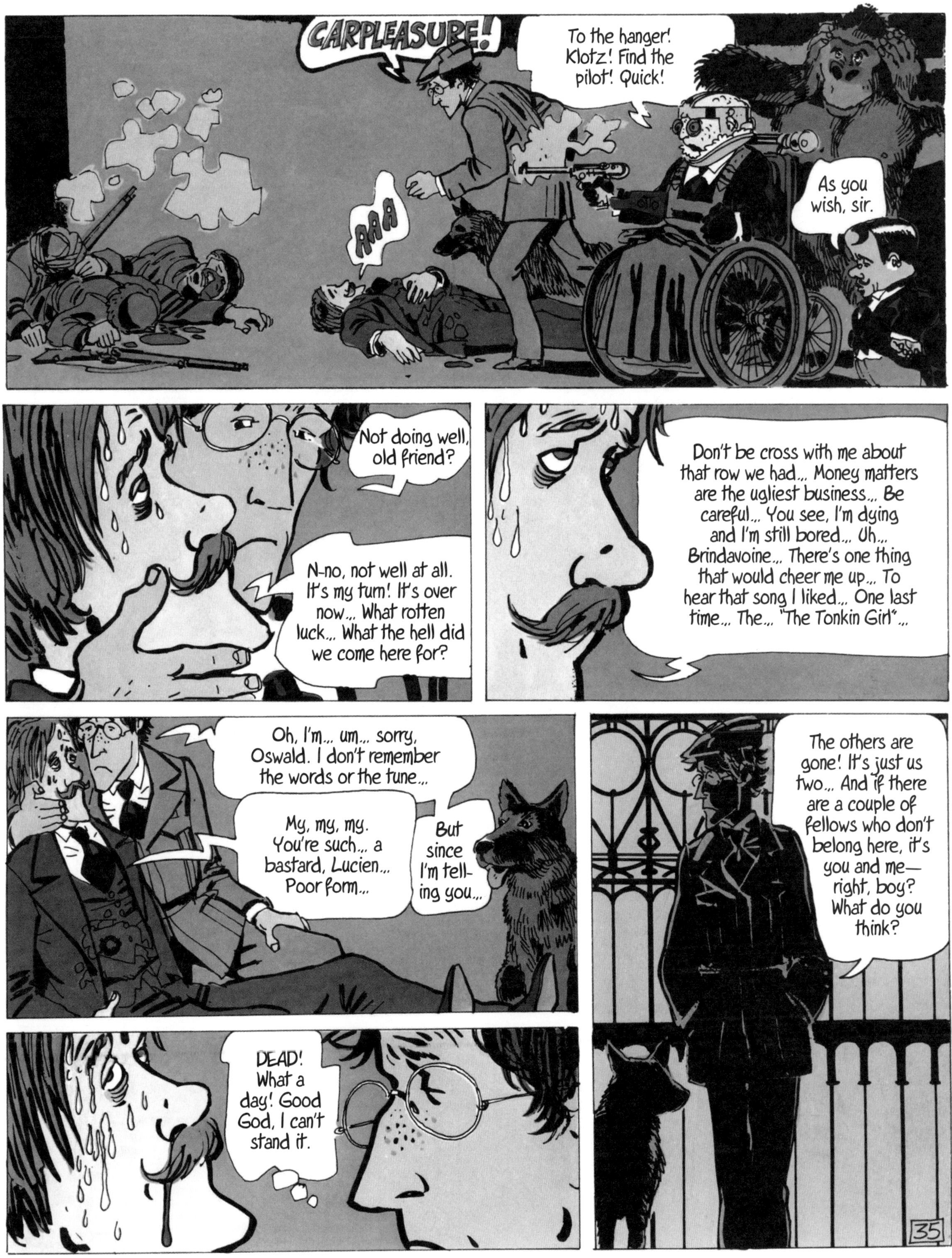
CARPLEASURE!
To the hanger! Klotz! Find the pilot! Quick!
AAA
As you wish, sir.
Not doing well, old friend?
N-no, not well at all. It's my turn! It's over now... What rotten luck... What the hell did we come here for?
Don't be cross with me about that row we had... Money matters are the ugliest business... Be careful... You see, I'm dying and I'm still bored... Uh... Brindavoine... There's one thing that would cheer me up... To hear that song I liked... One last time... The... "The Tonkin Girl"...
Oh, I'm... um... sorry, Oswald. I don't remember the words or the tune...
My, my, my. You're such... a bastard, Lucien... Poor form...
But since I'm telling you...
The others are gone! It's just us two... And if there are a couple of fellows who don't belong here, it's you and me—right, boy? What do you think?
DEAD! What a day! Good God, I can't stand it.
35

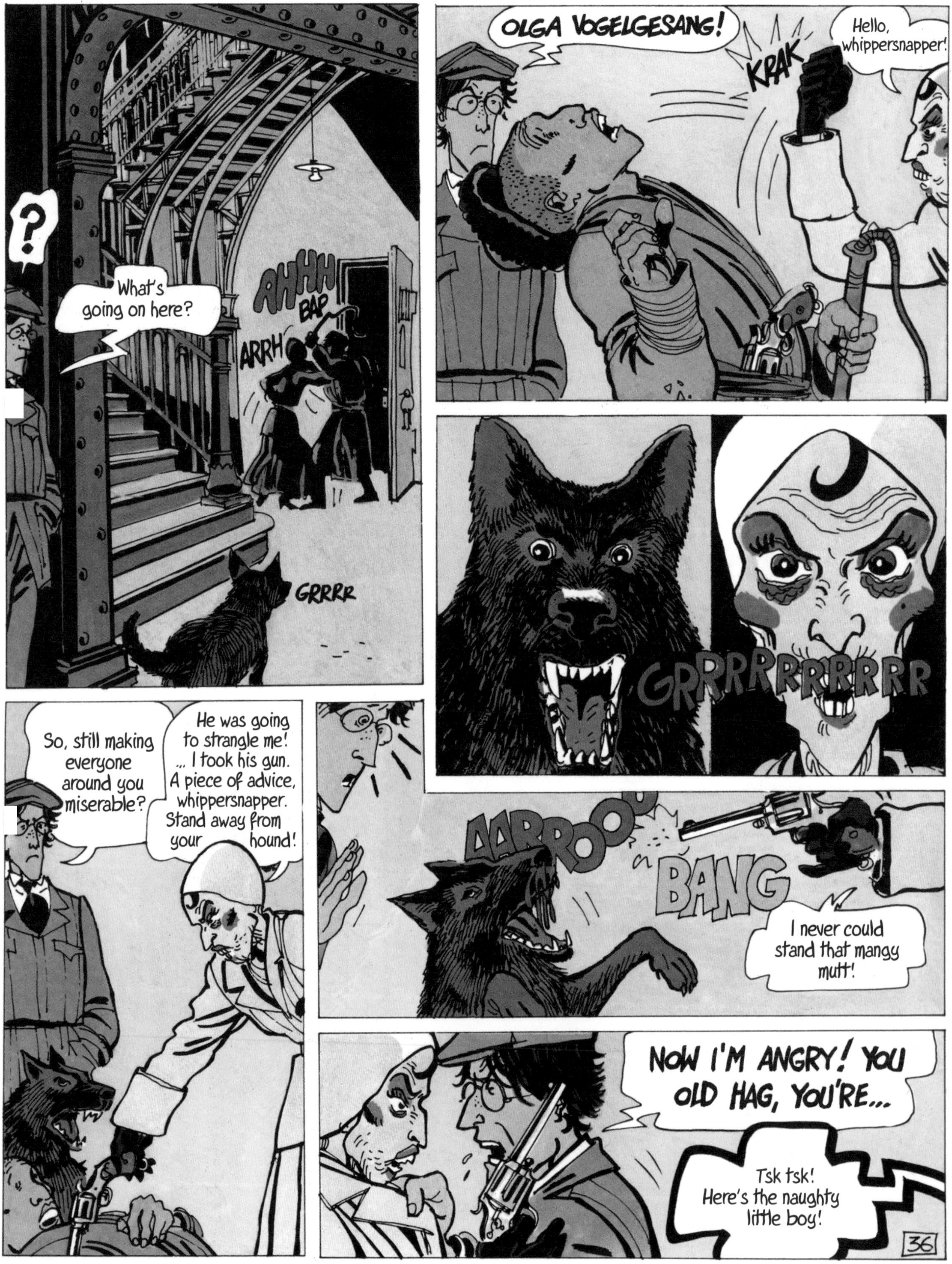
?
What's going on here?
AHHH
BAP
ARRH
GRRRR
OLGA VOGELGESANG!
KRAK
Hello, whippersnapper!
GRRRRRRRRRRR
So, still making everyone around you miserable?
He was going to strangle me! ... I took his gun. A piece of advice, whippersnapper. Stand away from your hound!
AARROOO
BANG
I never could stand that mangy mutt!
NOW I'M ANGRY! YOU OLD HAG, YOU'RE...
Tsk tsk! Here's the naughty little boy!
36

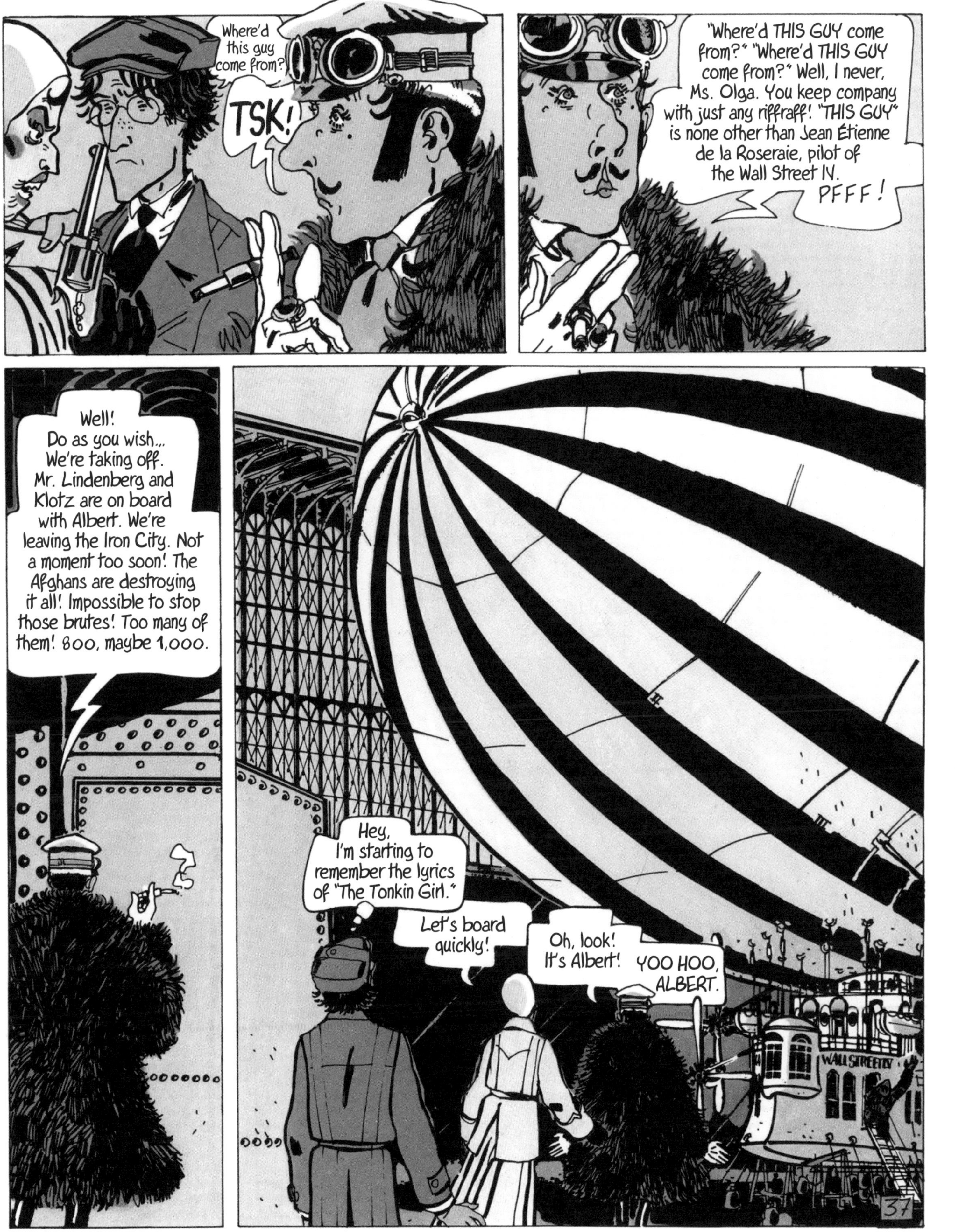
Where'd this guy come from?
TSK!
"Where'd THIS GUY come from?" "Where'd THIS GUY come from?" Well, I never, Ms. Olga. You keep company with just any riffraff! "THIS GUY" is none other than Jean Étienne de la Roseraie, pilot of the Wall Street IV.
PFFF!
Well! Do as you wish... We're taking off. Mr. Lindenberg and Klotz are on board with Albert. We're leaving the Iron City. Not a moment too soon! The Afghans are destroying it all! Impossible to stop those brutes! Too many of them! 800, maybe 1,000.
Hey, I'm starting to remember the lyrics of "The Tonkin Girl."
Let's board quickly!
Oh, look! It's Albert!
YOO HOO, ALBERT.
WALL STREET IV
37

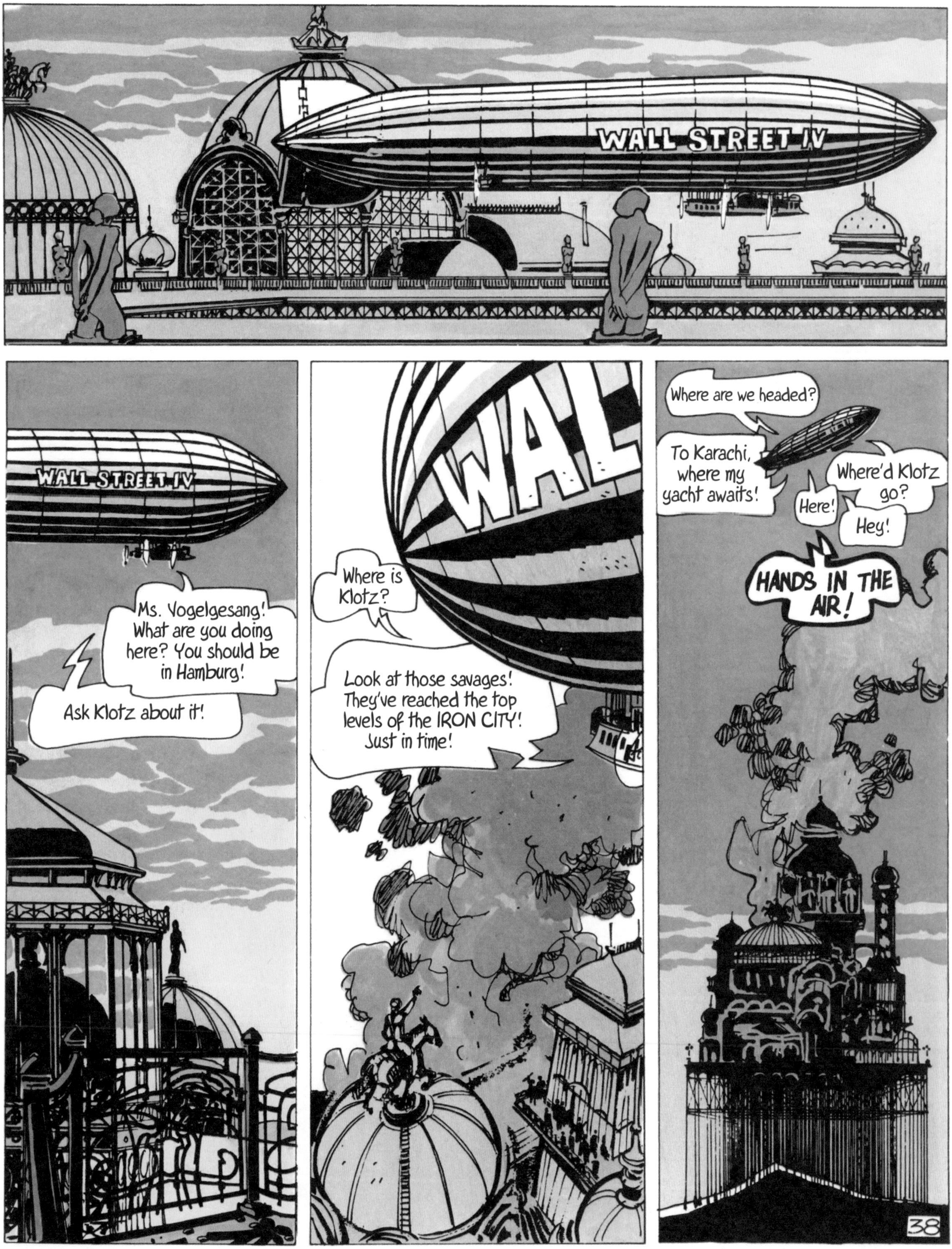
WALL STREET IV
WALL STREET IV
Ms. Vogelgesang! What are you doing here? You should be in Hamburg!
Ask Klotz about it!
WAL
Where is Klotz?
Look at those savages! They've reached the top levels of the IRON CITY! Just in time!
Where are we headed?
To Karachi, where my yacht awaits!
Where'd Klotz go?
Here!
Hey!
HANDS IN THE AIR!
38

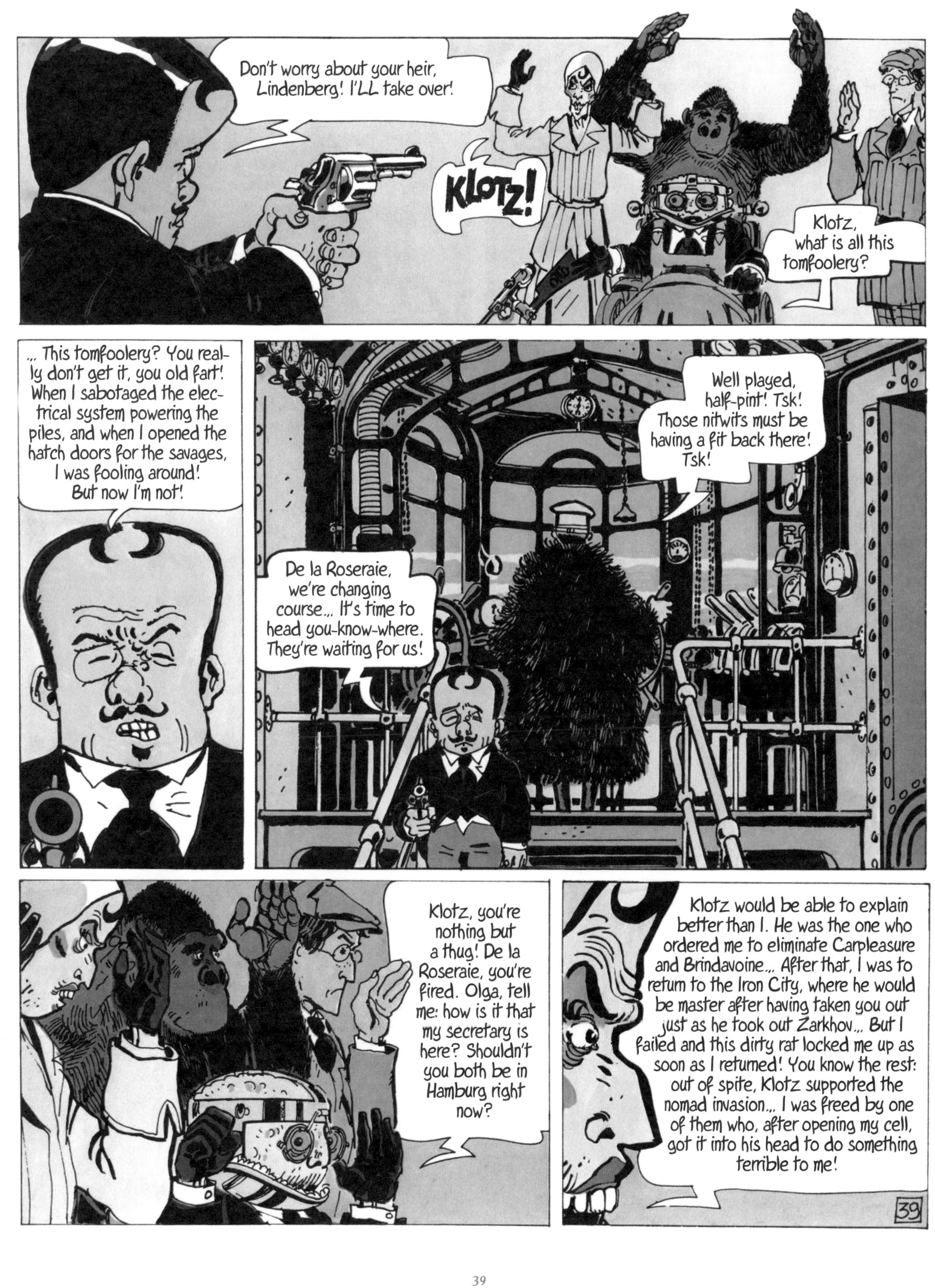
Don't worry about your heir, Lindenberg! I'LL take over!
KLOTZ!
Klotz, what is all this tomfoolery?
... This tomfoolery? You really don't get it, you old fart! When I sabotaged the electrical system powering the piles, and when I opened the hatch doors for the savages, I was fooling around! But now I'm not!
Well played, half-pint! Tsk! Those nitwits must be having a fit back there! Tsk!
De la Roseraie, we're changing course... It's time to head you-know-where. They're waiting for us!
Klotz, you're nothing but a thug! De la Roseraie, you're fired. Olga, tell me: how is it that my secretary is here? Shouldn't you both be in Hamburg right now?
Klotz would be able to explain better than I. He was the one who ordered me to eliminate Carpleasure and Brindavoine... After that, I was to return to the Iron City, where he would be master after having taken you out just as he took out Zarkhov... But I failed and this dirty rat locked me up as soon as I returned! You know the rest: out of spite, Klotz supported the nomad invasion... I was freed by one of them who, after opening my cell, got it into his head to do something terrible to me!
39

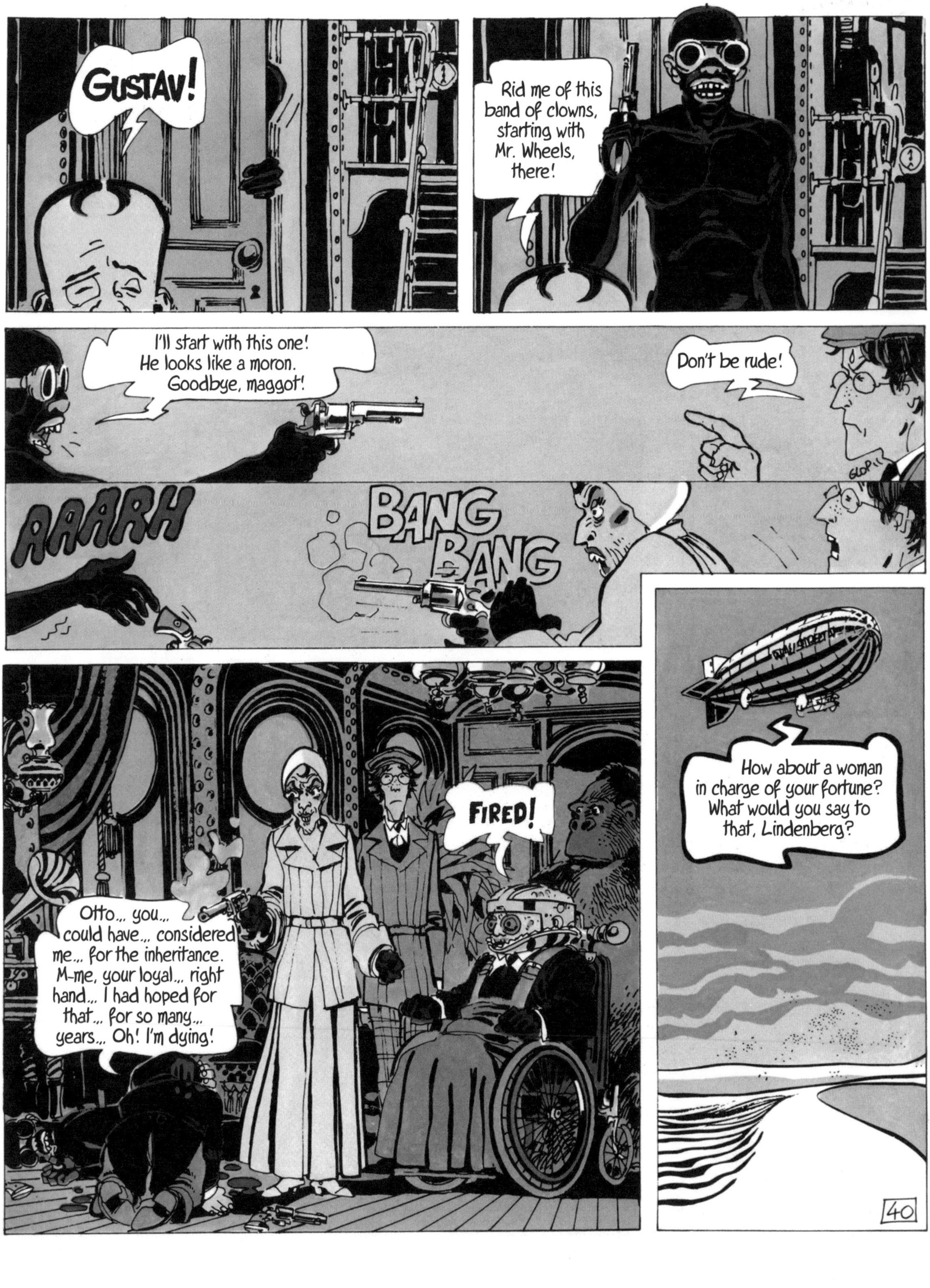
GUSTAV!
Rid me of this band of clowns, starting with Mr. Wheels, there!
I'll start with this one! He looks like a moron. Goodbye, maggot!
Don't be rude!
GLOP...
AAARH
BANG
BANG
How about a woman in charge of your fortune? What would you say to that, Lindenberg?
FIRED!
Otto... you... could have... considered me... for the inheritance. M-me, your loyal... right hand... I had hoped for that... for so many... years... Oh! I'm dying!
40

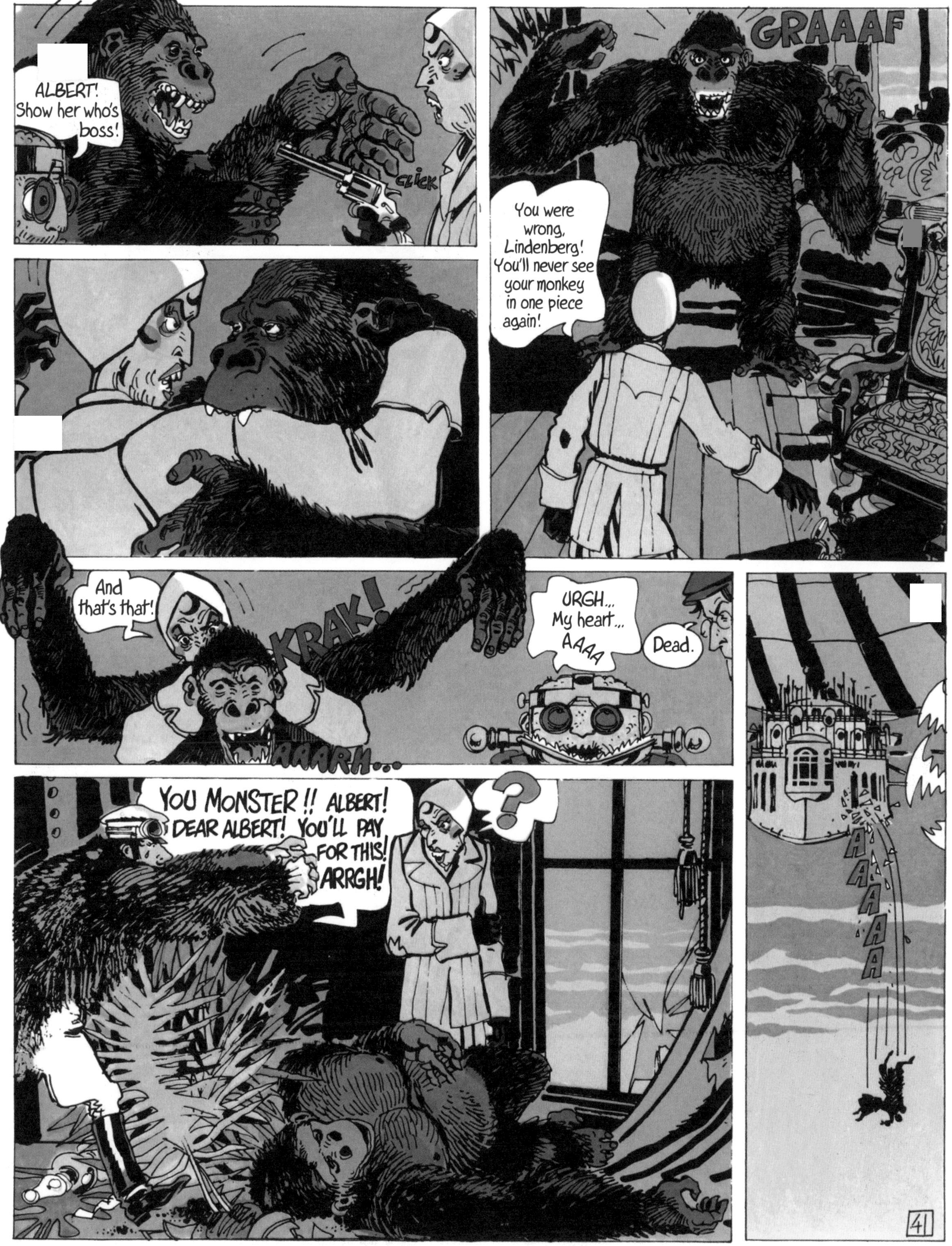

ALBERT! Show her who's boss!
CLICK
GRAAAF
You were wrong, Lindenberg! You'll never see your monkey in one piece again!
And that's that!
KRAK!
RAARH...
URGH... My heart... AAAA
Dead.
YOU MONSTER!! ALBERT! DEAR ALBERT! YOU'LL PAY FOR THIS! ARRGH!
?
AAAAAAA
41

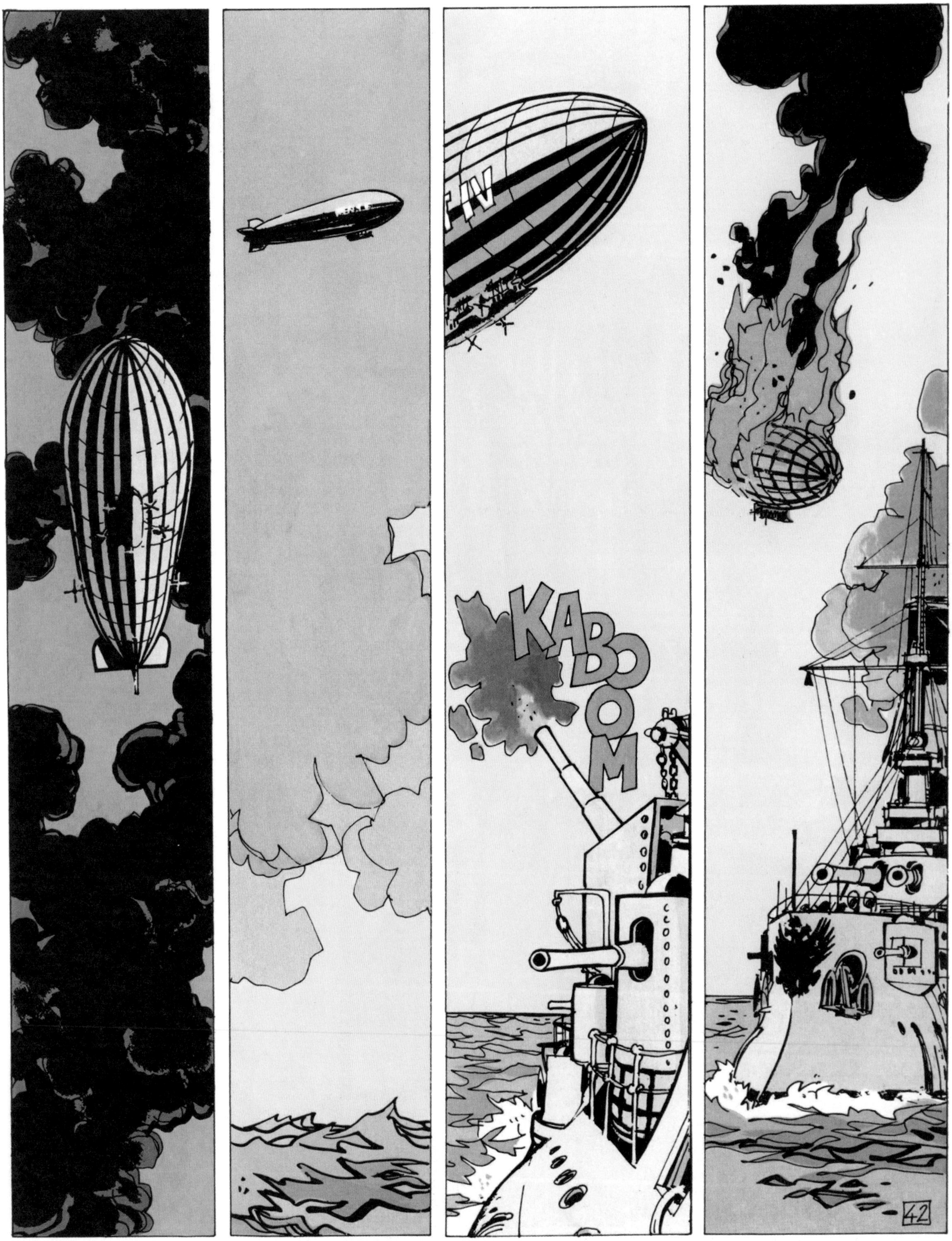
KABOOM
42

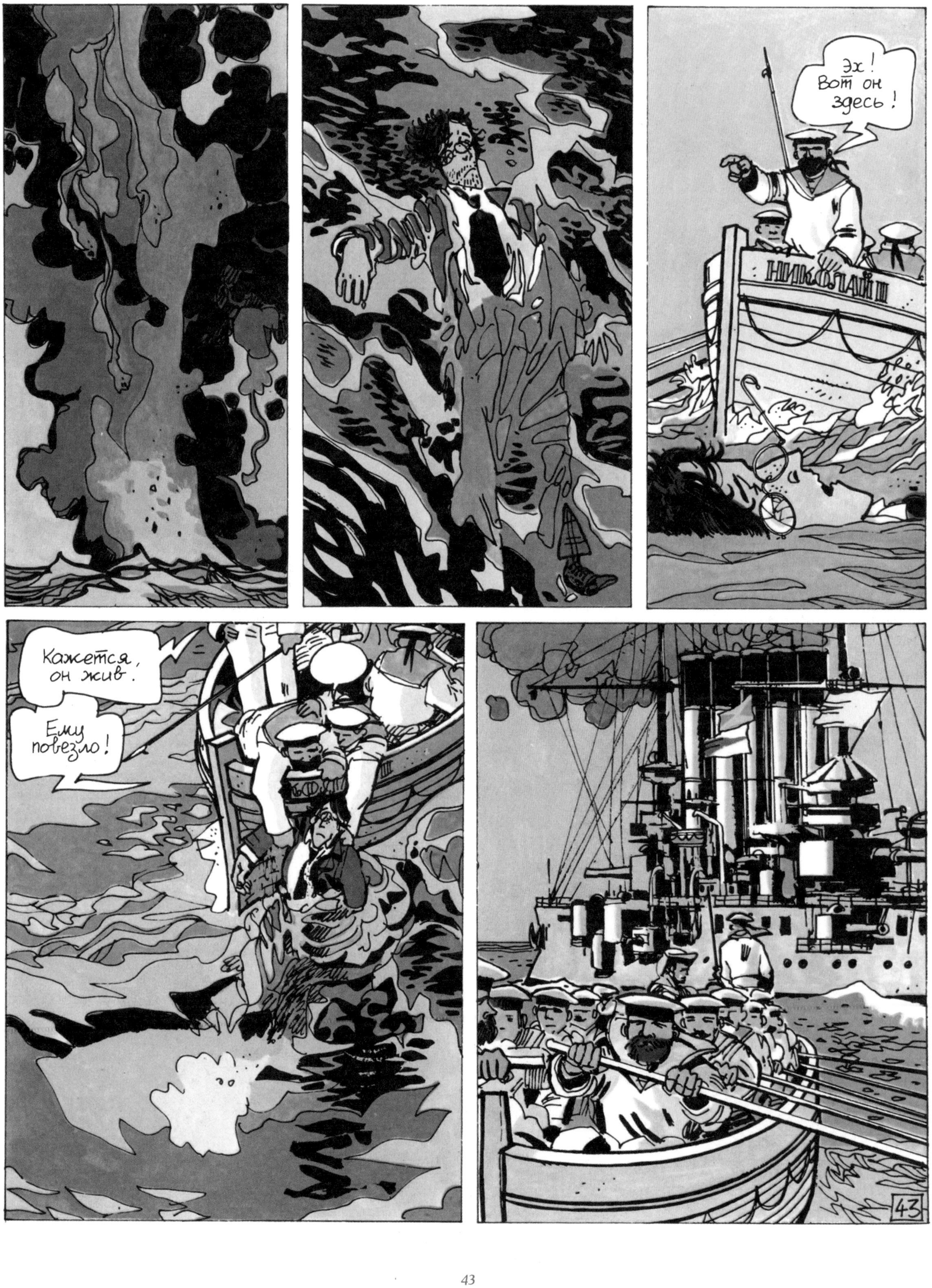
Эх! Вот он здесь!
НИКОЛАЙ II
Кажется, он жив.
Ему повезло!
43

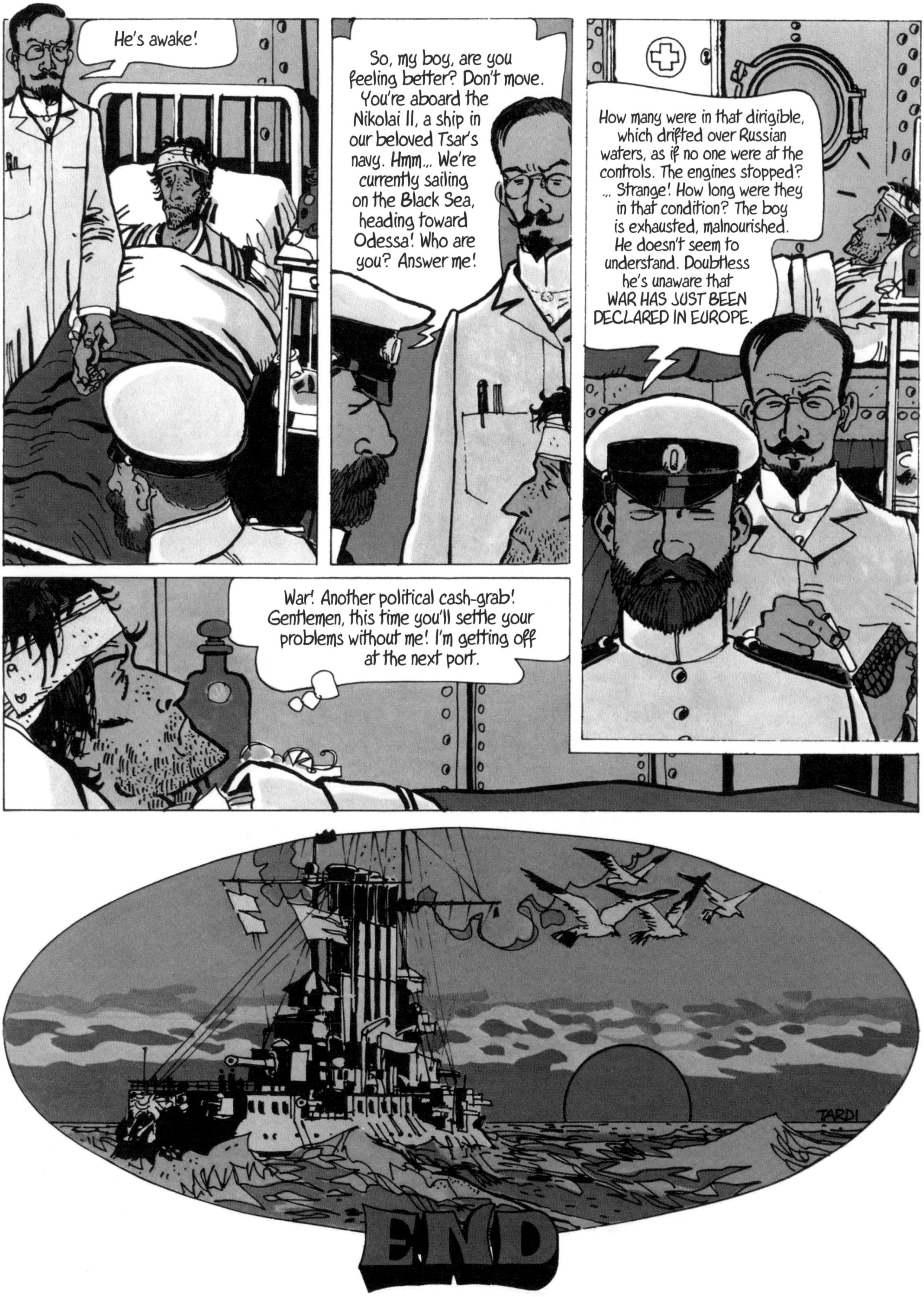
He's awake!
So, my boy, are you feeling better? Don't move. You're aboard the Nikolai II, a ship in our beloved Tsar's navy. Hmm... We're currently sailing on the Black Sea, heading toward Odessa! Who are you? Answer me!
How many were in that dirigible, which drifted over Russian waters, as if no one were at the controls. The engines stopped? ... Strange! How long were they in that condition? The boy is exhausted, malnourished. He doesn't seem to understand. Doubtless he's unaware that WAR HAS JUST BEEN DECLARED IN EUROPE.
War! Another political cash-grab! Gentlemen, this time you'll settle your problems without me! I'm getting off at the next port.
TARDI
END

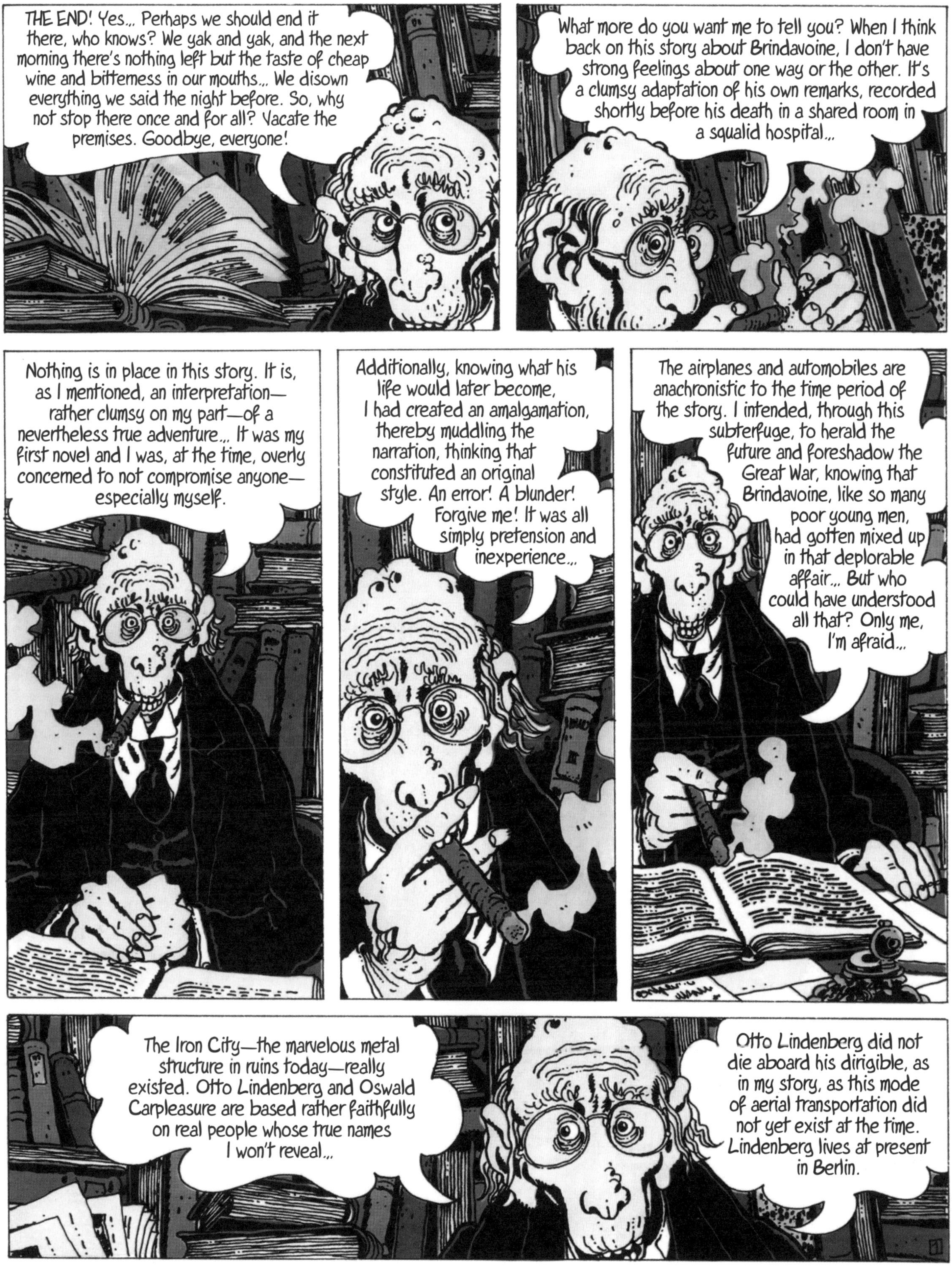
THE END! Yes... Perhaps we should end it there, who knows? We yak and yak, and the next morning there's nothing left but the taste of cheap wine and bitterness in our mouths... We disown everything we said the night before. So, why not stop there once and for all? Vacate the premises. Goodbye, everyone!
What more do you want me to tell you? When I think back on this story about Brindavoine, I don't have strong feelings about one way or the other. It's a clumsy adaptation of his own remarks, recorded shortly before his death in a shared room in a squalid hospital...
Nothing is in place in this story. It is, as I mentioned, an interpretation—rather clumsy on my part—of a nevertheless true adventure... It was my first novel and I was, at the time, overly concerned to not compromise anyone—especially myself.
Additionally, knowing what his life would later become, I had created an amalgamation, thereby muddling the narration, thinking that constituted an original style. An error! A blunder! Forgive me! It was all simply pretension and inexperience...
The airplanes and automobiles are anachronistic to the time period of the story. I intended, through this subterfuge, to herald the future and foreshadow the Great War, knowing that Brindavoine, like so many poor young men, had gotten mixed up in that deplorable affair... But who could have understood all that? Only me, I'm afraid...
The Iron City—the marvelous metal structure in ruins today—really existed. Otto Lindenberg and Oswald Carpleasure are based rather faithfully on real people whose true names I won't reveal...
Otto Lindenberg did not die aboard his dirigible, as in my story, as this mode of aerial transportation did not yet exist at the time. Lindenberg lives at present in Berlin.

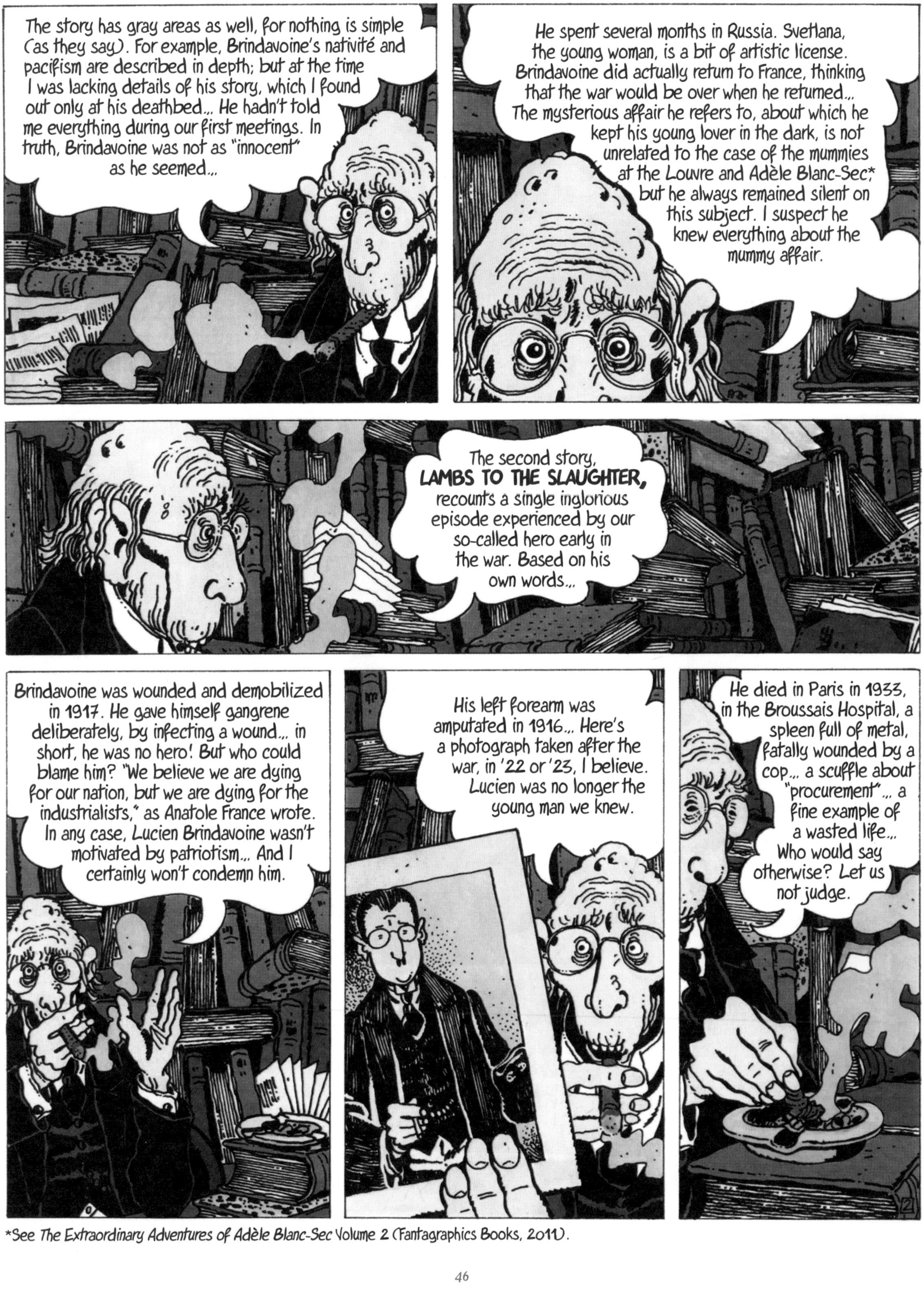
The story has gray areas as well, for nothing is simple (as they say). For example, Brindavoine's nativité and pacifism are described in depth; but at the time I was lacking details of his story, which I found out only at his deathbed... He hadn't told me everything during our first meetings. In truth, Brindavoine was not as "innocent" as he seemed...
He spent several months in Russia. Svetlana, the young woman, is a bit of artistic license. Brindavoine did actually return to France, thinking that the war would be over when he returned... The mysterious affair he refers to, about which he kept his young lover in the dark, is not unrelated to the case of the mummies at the Louvre and Adèle Blanc-Sec* but he always remained silent on this subject. I suspect he knew everything about the mummy affair.
The second story, **LAMBS TO THE SLAUGHTER,** recounts a single inglorious episode experienced by our so-called hero early in the war. Based on his own words...
Brindavoine was wounded and demobilized in 1917. He gave himself gangrene deliberately, by infecting a wound... in short, he was no hero! But who could blame him? "We believe we are dying for our nation, but we are dying for the industrialists," as Anatole France wrote. In any case, Lucien Brindavoine wasn't motivated by patriotism... And I certainly won't condemn him.
His left forearm was amputated in 1916... Here's a photograph taken after the war, in '22 or '23, I believe. Lucien was no longer the young man we knew.
He died in Paris in 1933, in the Broussais Hospital, a spleen full of metal, fatally wounded by a cop... a scuffle about "procurement"... a fine example of a wasted life... Who would say otherwise? Let us not judge.
2

*See *The Extraordinary Adventures of Adèle Blanc-Sec* Volume 2 (Fantagraphics Books, 2011).

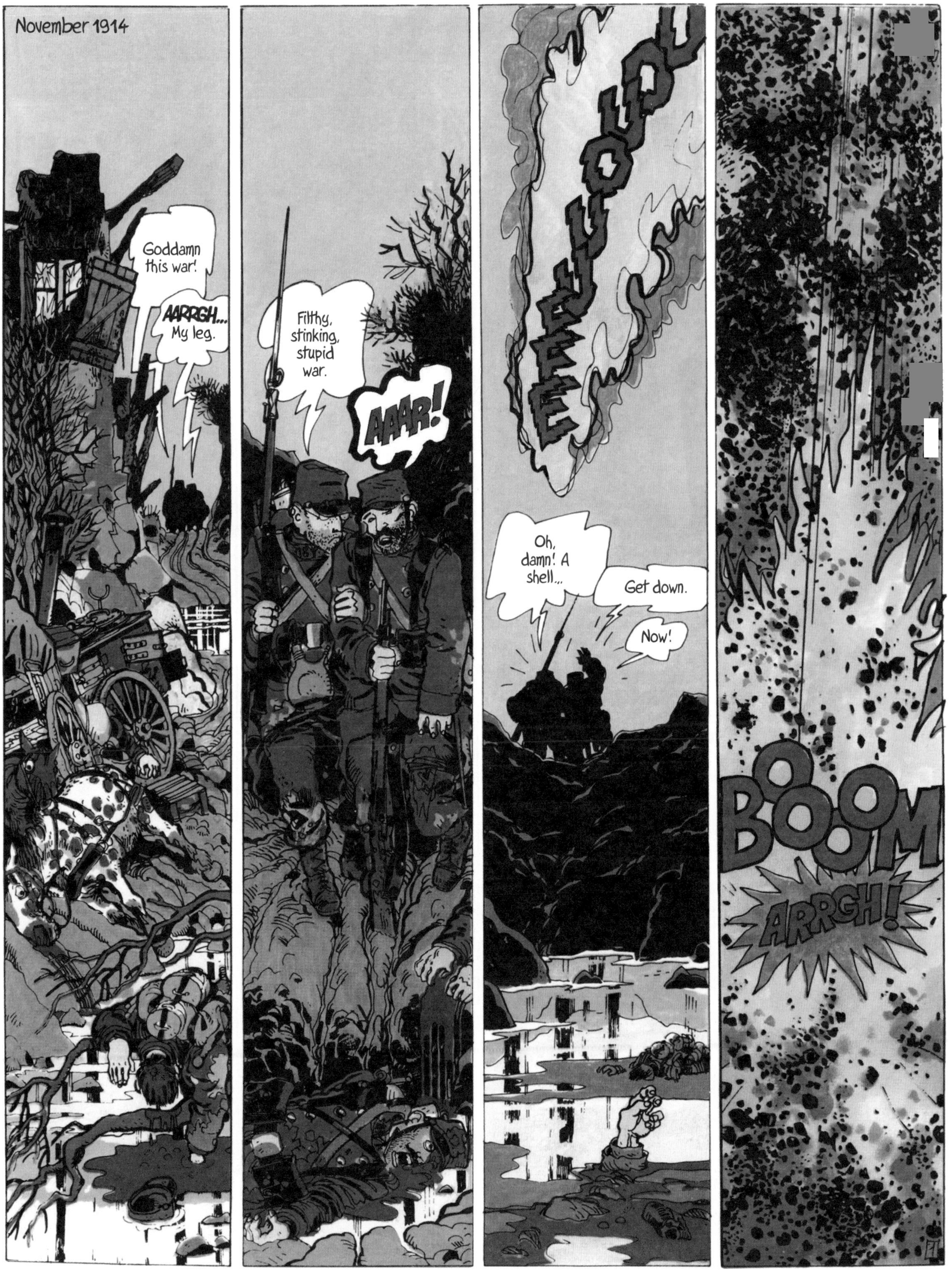
November 1914
Goddamn this war!
AARRGH... My leg.
Filthy, stinking, stupid war.
AAAR!
Oh, damn! A shell...
Get down.
Now!
BOOOOM
ARRGH!

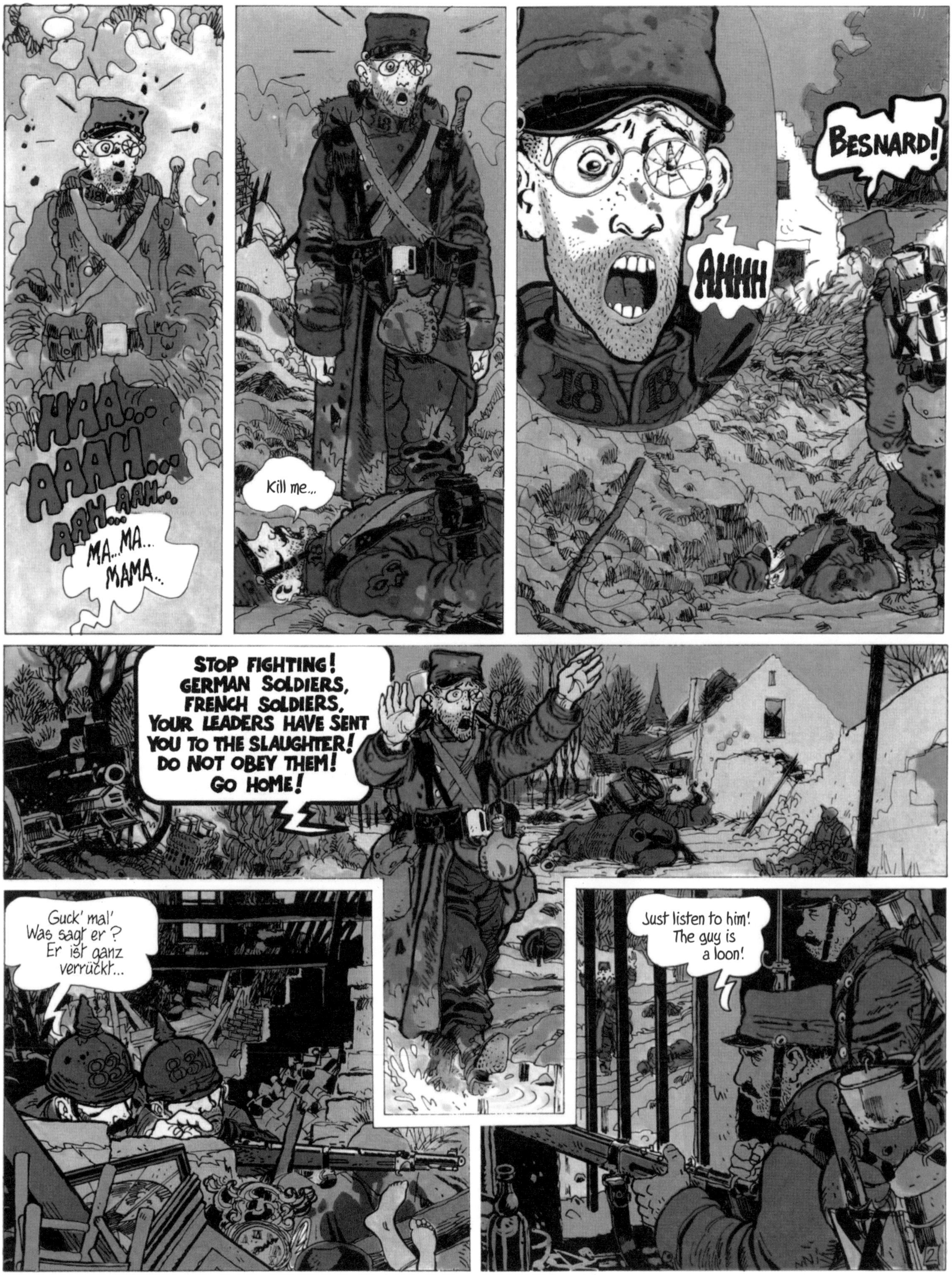
HAA... AAAH... AAH... AAH...
MA...MA... MAMA...
Kill me...
BESNARD!
AHHH
STOP FIGHTING! GERMAN SOLDIERS, FRENCH SOLDIERS, YOUR LEADERS HAVE SENT YOU TO THE SLAUGHTER! DO NOT OBEY THEM! GO HOME!
Guck' mal' Was sagt er? Er ist ganz verrückt...
Just listen to him! The guy is a loon!

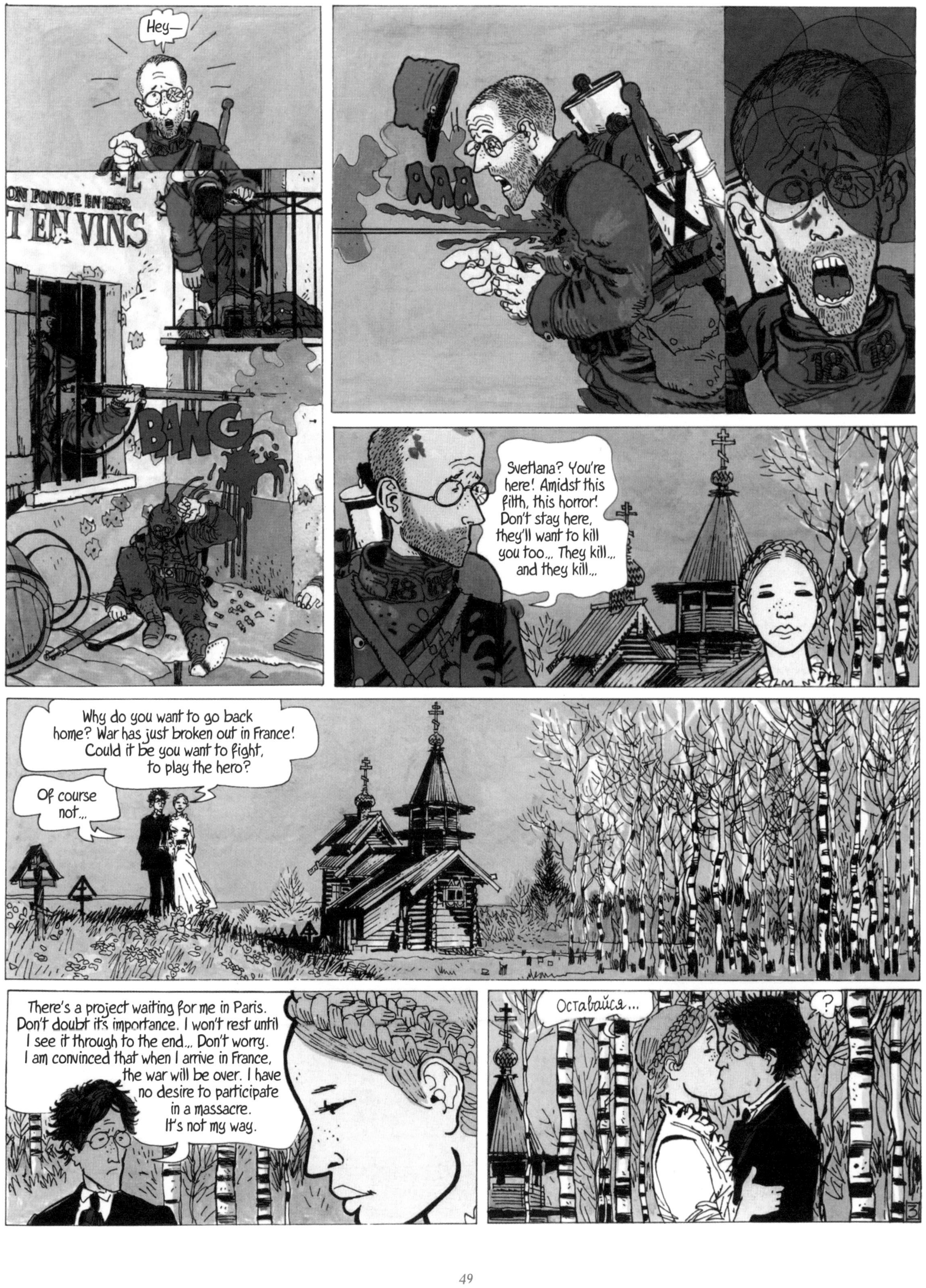
Hey—
ON FONDEE EN 1882
T EN VINS
BANG
AAA
Svetlana? You're here! Amidst this filth, this horror! Don't stay here, they'll want to kill you too... They kill... and they kill...
Why do you want to go back home? War has just broken out in France! Could it be you want to fight, to play the hero?
Of course not...
There's a project waiting for me in Paris. Don't doubt its importance. I won't rest until I see it through to the end... Don't worry. I am convinced that when I arrive in France, the war will be over. I have no desire to participate in a massacre. It's not my way.
Оставайся...
?

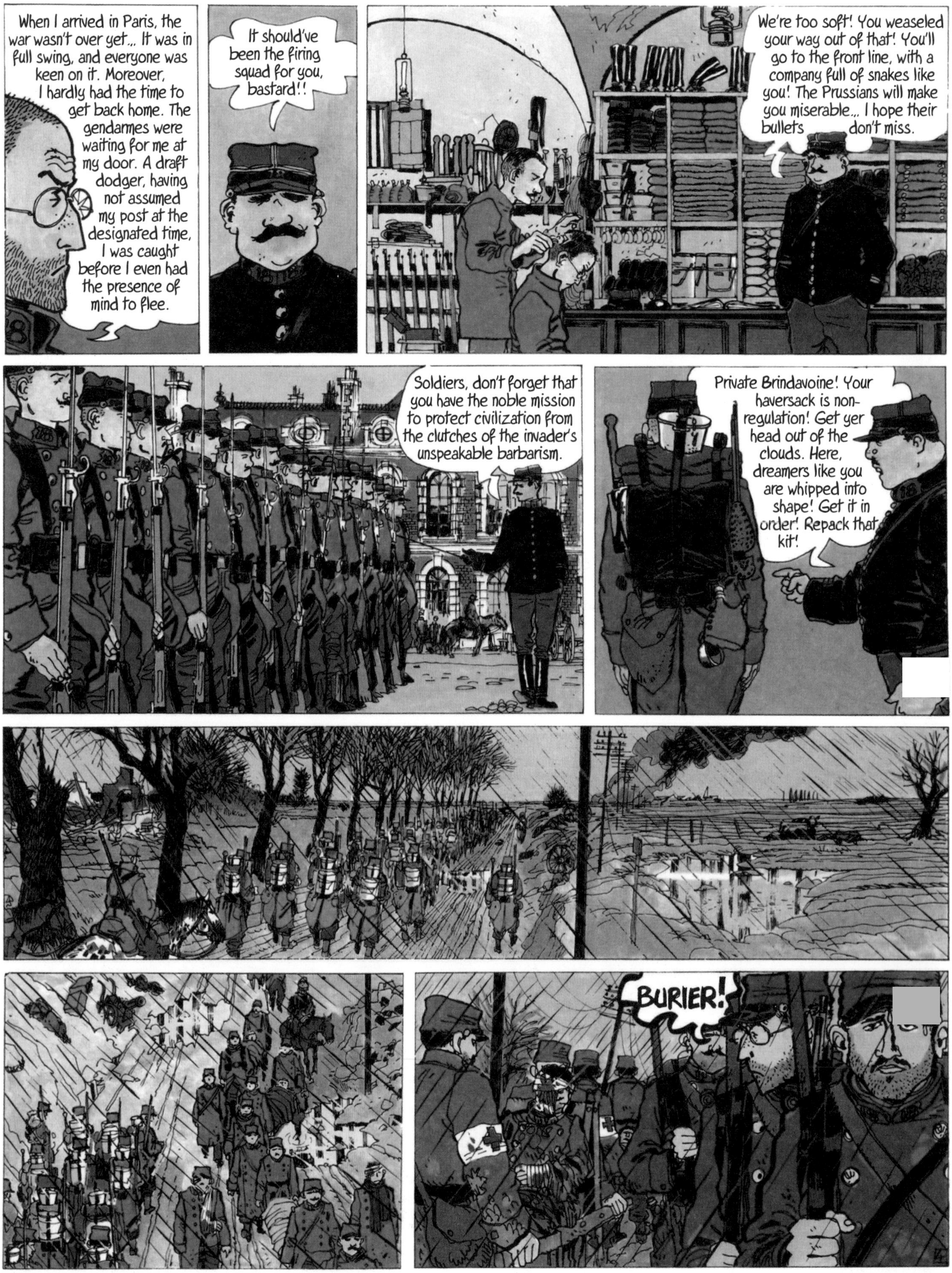
When I arrived in Paris, the war wasn't over yet... It was in full swing, and everyone was keen on it. Moreover, I hardly had the time to get back home. The gendarmes were waiting for me at my door. A draft dodger, having not assumed my post at the designated time, I was caught before I even had the presence of mind to flee.
It should've been the firing squad for you, bastard!!
We're too soft! You weaseled your way out of that! You'll go to the front line, with a company full of snakes like you! The Prussians will make you miserable... I hope their bullets don't miss.
Soldiers, don't forget that you have the noble mission to protect civilization from the clutches of the invader's unspeakable barbarism.
Private Brindavoine! Your haversack is non-regulation! Get yer head out of the clouds. Here, dreamers like you are whipped into shape! Get it in order! Repack that kit!
BURIER!

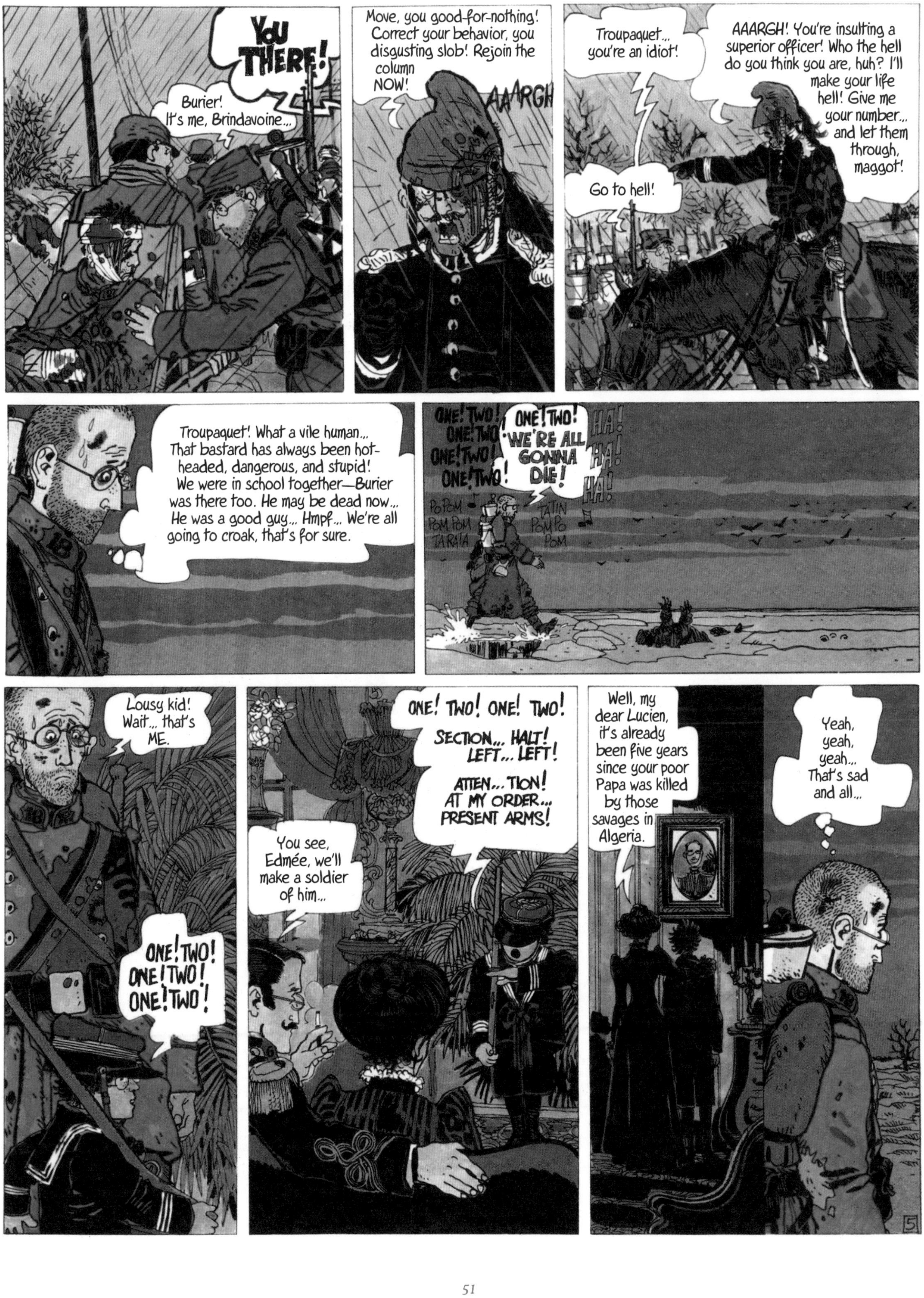
YOU THERE!
Burier! It's me, Brindavoine...
Move, you good-for-nothing! Correct your behavior, you disgusting slob! Rejoin the column NOW!
AAARGH
Troupaquet... you're an idiot!
AAARGH! You're insulting a superior officer! Who the hell do you think you are, huh? I'll make your life hell! Give me your number... and let them through, maggot!
Go to hell!
Troupaquet! What a vile human... That bastard has always been hot-headed, dangerous, and stupid! We were in school together—Burier was there too. He may be dead now... He was a good guy... Hmpf... We're all going to croak, that's for sure.
ONE! TWO! ONE! TWO! ONE! TWO! ONE! TWO!
ONE! TWO! WE'RE ALL GONNA DIE!
HA! HA! HA!
POPOM POM POM TARATA
TATIN POM PO POM
Lousy kid! Wait... that's ME.
ONE! TWO! ONE! TWO! ONE! TWO!
ONE! TWO! ONE! TWO!
SECTION... HALT! LEFT... LEFT!
ATTEN... TION! AT MY ORDER... PRESENT ARMS!
You see, Edmée, we'll make a soldier of him...
Well, my dear Lucien, it's already been five years since your poor Papa was killed by those savages in Algeria.
Yeah, yeah, yeah... That's sad and all...
5

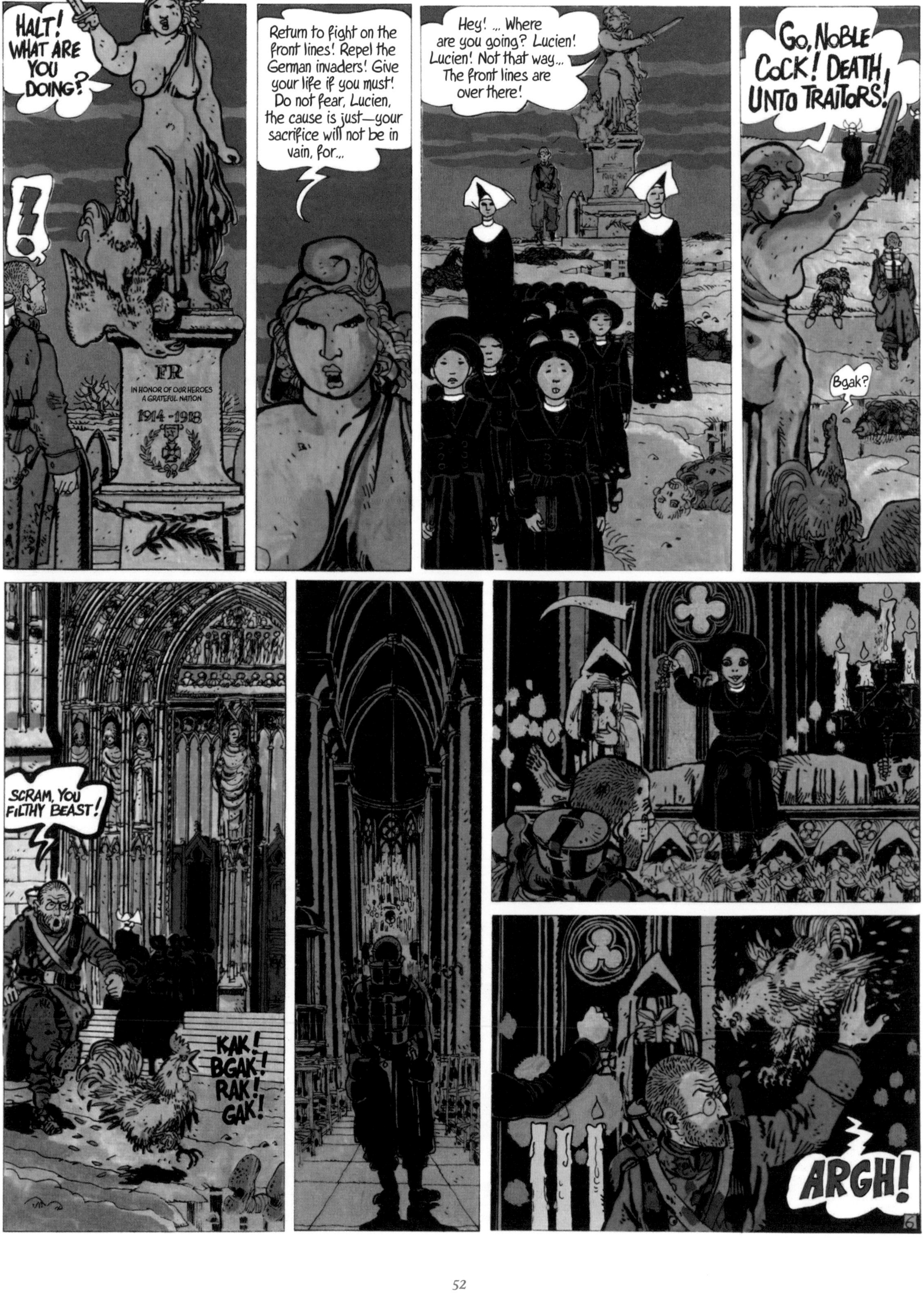
HALT! WHAT ARE YOU DOING?
!
FR
IN HONOR OF OUR HEROES
A GRATEFUL NATION
1914-1918
Return to fight on the front lines! Repel the German invaders! Give your life if you must! Do not fear, Lucien, the cause is just—your sacrifice will not be in vain, for...
Hey! ... Where are you going? Lucien! Lucien! Not that way... The front lines are over there!
GO, NOBLE COCK! DEATH UNTO TRAITORS!
Bgak?
SCRAM, YOU FILTHY BEAST!
KAK! BGAK! RAK! GAK!
ARGH!
6

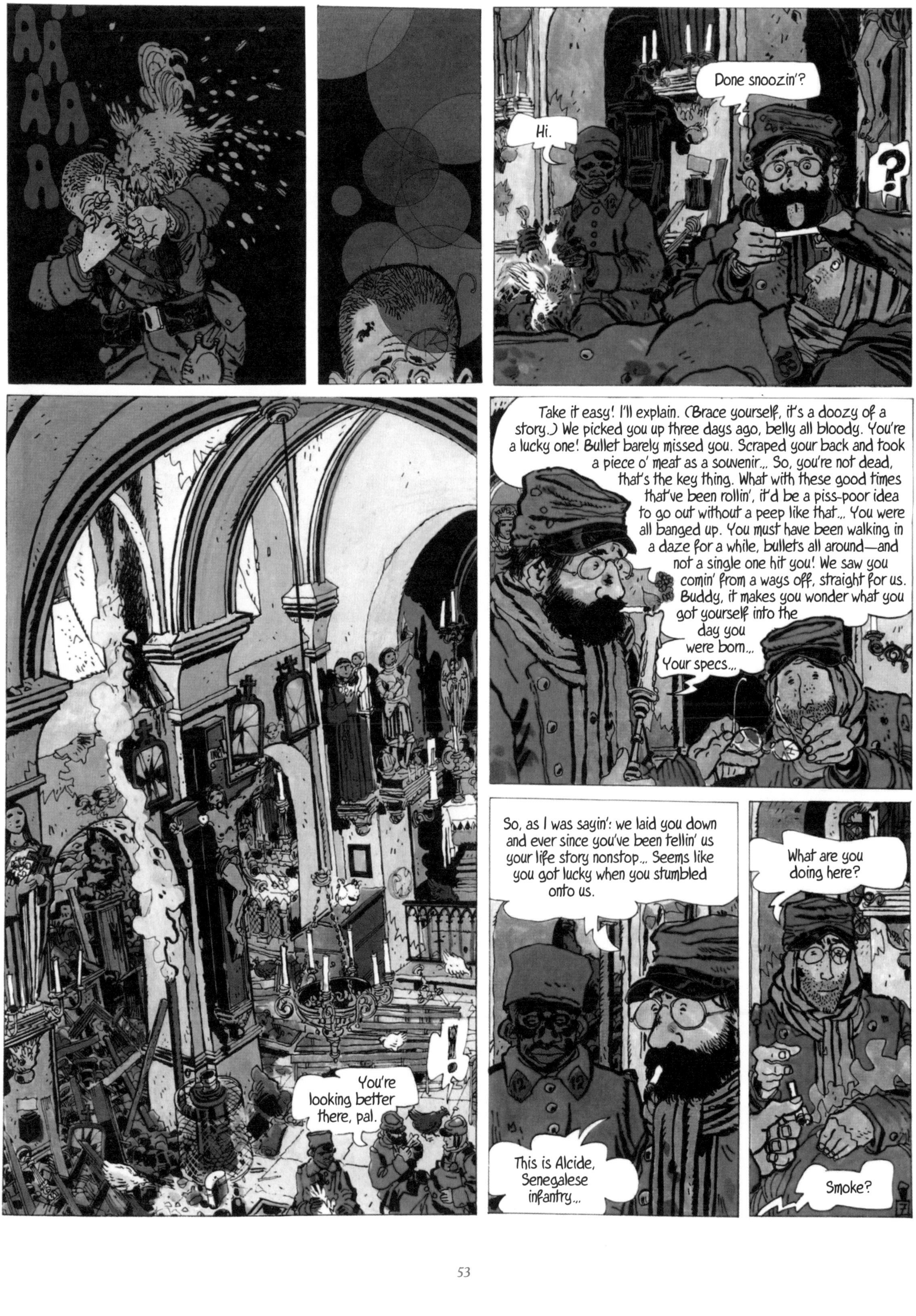
Done snoozin'?
Hi.
?
You're looking better there, pal.
!
Take it easy! I'll explain. (Brace yourself, it's a doozy of a story.) We picked you up three days ago, belly all bloody. You're a lucky one! Bullet barely missed you. Scraped your back and took a piece o' meat as a souvenir... So, you're not dead, that's the key thing. What with these good times that've been rollin', it'd be a piss-poor idea to go out without a peep like that... You were all banged up. You must have been walking in a daze for a while, bullets all around—and not a single one hit you! We saw you comin' from a ways off, straight for us. Buddy, it makes you wonder what you got yourself into the day you were born...
Your specs...
So, as I was sayin': we laid you down and ever since you've been tellin' us your life story nonstop... Seems like you got lucky when you stumbled onto us.
This is Alcide, Senegalese infantry...
What are you doing here?
Smoke?

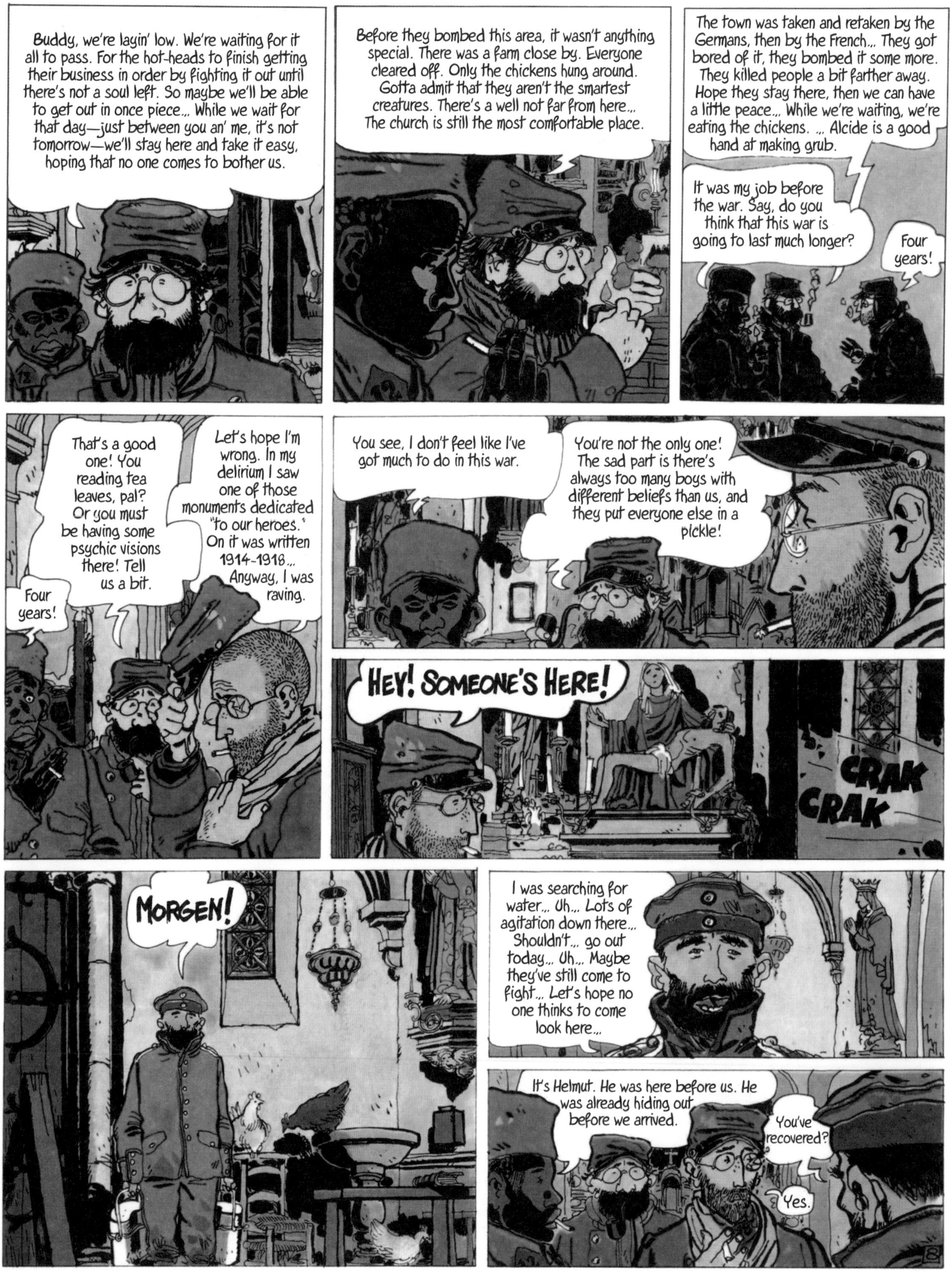

Buddy, we're layin' low. We're waiting for it all to pass. For the hot-heads to finish getting their business in order by fighting it out until there's not a soul left. So maybe we'll be able to get out in once piece... While we wait for that day—just between you an' me, it's not tomorrow—we'll stay here and take it easy, hoping that no one comes to bother us.
Before they bombed this area, it wasn't anything special. There was a farm close by. Everyone cleared off. Only the chickens hung around. Gotta admit that they aren't the smartest creatures. There's a well not far from here... The church is still the most comfortable place.
The town was taken and retaken by the Germans, then by the French... They got bored of it, they bombed it some more. They killed people a bit farther away. Hope they stay there, then we can have a little peace... While we're waiting, we're eating the chickens. ... Alcide is a good hand at making grub.
It was my job before the war. Say, do you think that this war is going to last much longer?
Four years!
Four years!
That's a good one! You reading tea leaves, pal? Or you must be having some psychic visions there! Tell us a bit.
Let's hope I'm wrong. In my delirium I saw one of those monuments dedicated "to our heroes." On it was written 1914-1918... Anyway, I was raving.
You see, I don't feel like I've got much to do in this war.
You're not the only one! The sad part is there's always too many boys with different beliefs than us, and they put everyone else in a pickle!
HEY! SOMEONE'S HERE!
CRAK
CRAK
MORGEN!
I was searching for water... Uh... Lots of agitation down there... Shouldn't... go out today... Uh... Maybe they've still come to fight... Let's hope no one thinks to come look here...
It's Helmut. He was here before us. He was already hiding out before we arrived.
You've recovered?
Yes.

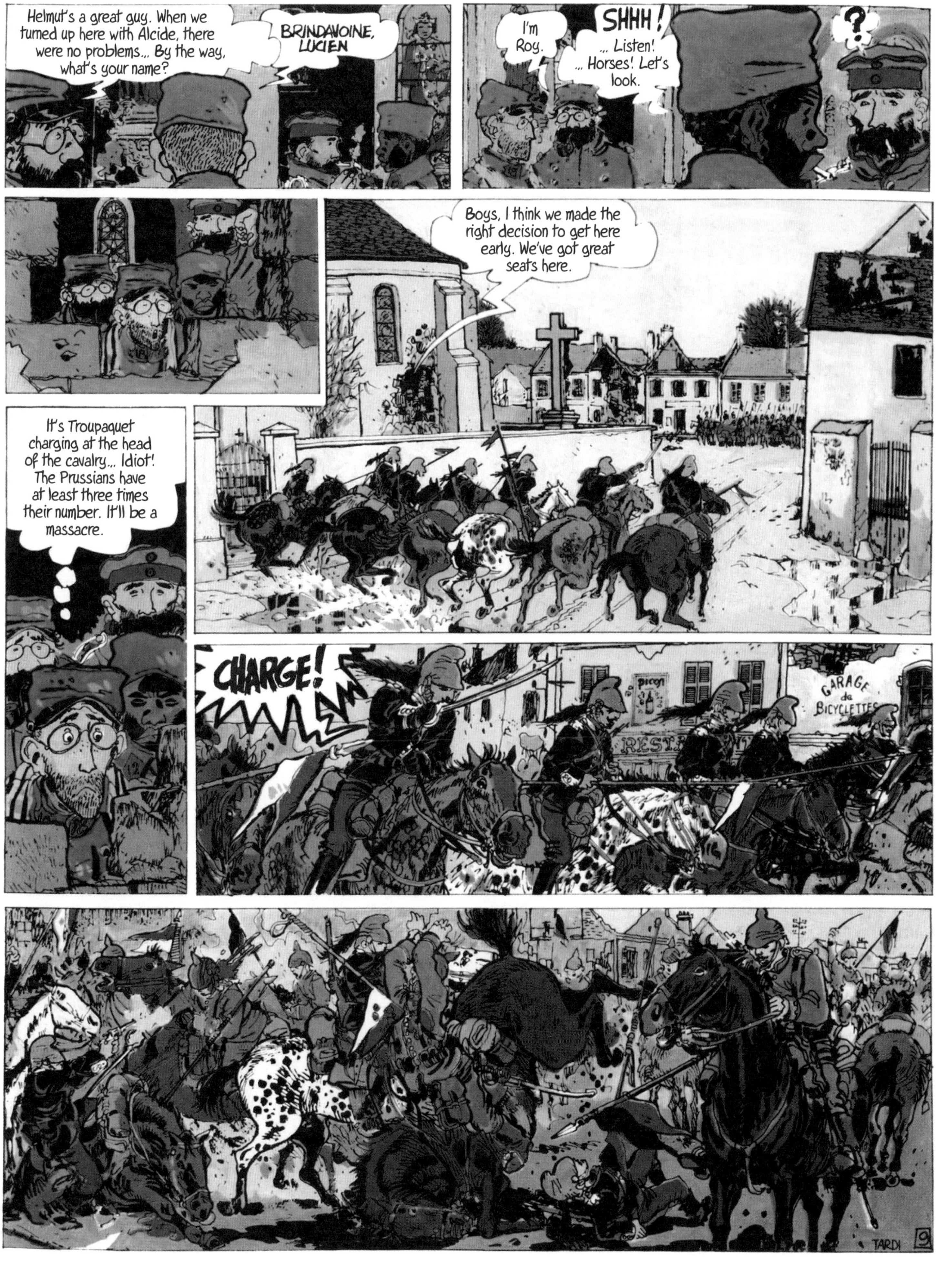

Helmut's a great guy. When we turned up here with Alcide, there were no problems... By the way, what's your name?
BRINDAVOINE, LUCIEN
I'm Roy.
SHHH!
... Listen! ... Horses! Let's look.
?
Boys, I think we made the right decision to get here early. We've got great seats here.
It's Troupaquet charging at the head of the cavalry... Idiot! The Prussians have at least three times their number. It'll be a massacre.
CHARGE!
PICON
GARAGE de BICYCLETTES
REST
TARDI
9

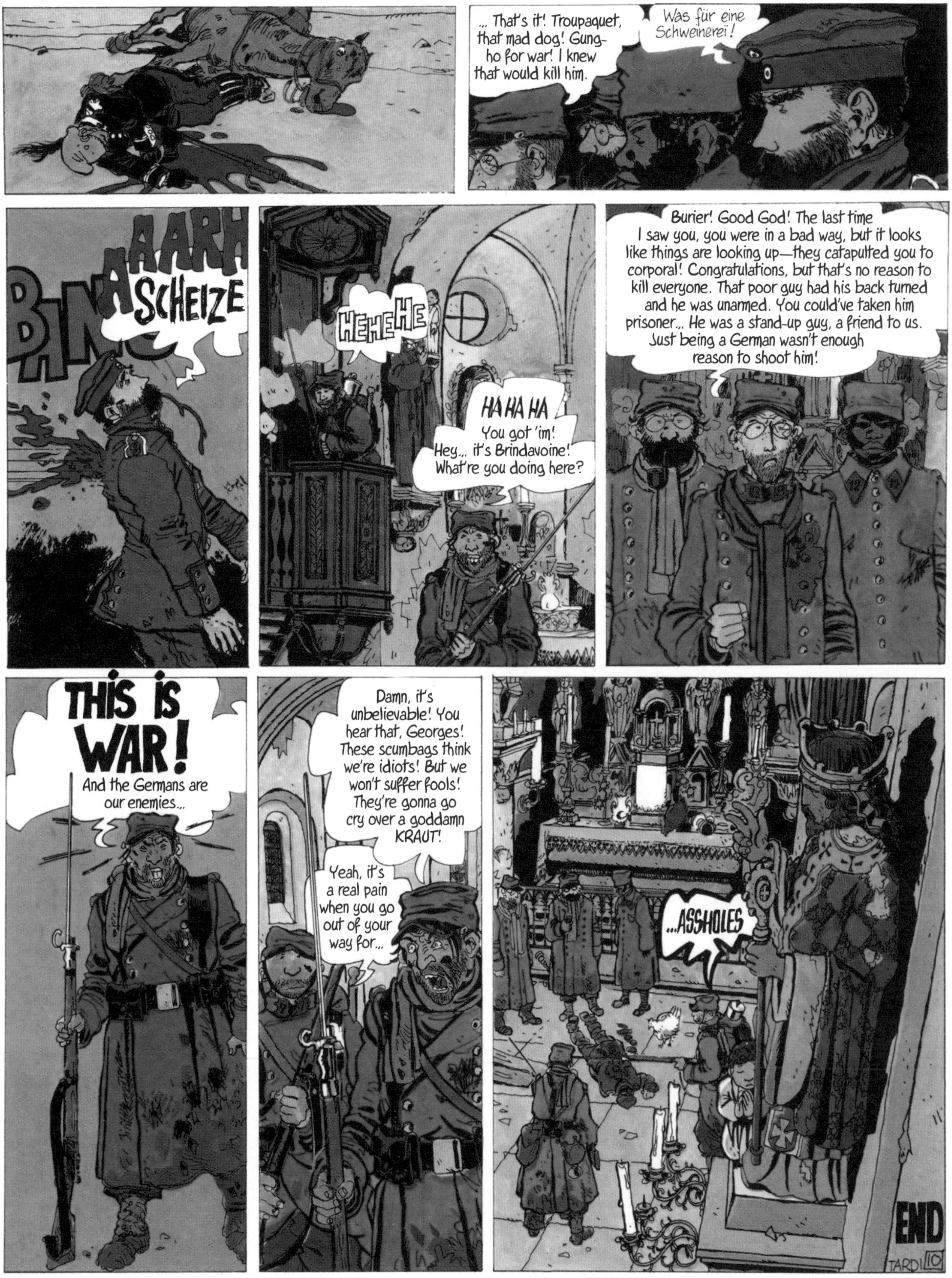

... That's it! Troupaquet, that mad dog! Gung-ho for war! I knew that would kill him.
Was für eine Schweinerei!
BANG
AARH
AARH
SCHEIZE
HEHEHEHE
HA HA HA
You got 'im! Hey... it's Brindavoine! What're you doing here?
Burier! Good God! The last time I saw you, you were in a bad way, but it looks like things are looking up—they catapulted you to corporal! Congratulations, but that's no reason to kill everyone. That poor guy had his back turned and he was unarmed. You could've taken him prisoner... He was a stand-up guy, a friend to us. Just being a German wasn't enough reason to shoot him!
THIS IS WAR!
And the Germans are our enemies...
Damn, it's unbelievable! You hear that, Georges! These scumbags think we're idiots! But we won't suffer fools! They're gonna go cry over a goddamn KRAUT!
Yeah, it's a real pain when you go out of your way for...
...ASSHOLES
END
TARDI 10

THE TARDI LIBRARY

 FANTAGRAPHICS BOOKS, INC.
7563 Lake City Way NE
Seattle, WA 98115

WWW.FANTAGRAPHICS.COM
FACEBOOK.COM/FANTAGRAPHICS
@FANTAGRAPHICS

TRANSLATOR: Jenna Allen
EDITOR: Conrad Groth
DESIGNER: Chelsea Wirtz
PRODUCTION: Christina Hwang
PUBLICITY: Jacq Cohen
ASSOCIATE PUBLISHER: Eric Reynolds
PUBLISHER: Gary Groth

This edition of *Farewell, Brindavoine* is copyright © 2021 Fantagraphics Books, Inc. *Adieu Brindavoine* copyright © 2011 Casterman. Translation copyright © 2021 Jenna Allen. Preface copyright © 2021 Benoît Mouchart. All rights reserved. Permission to reproduce content must be obtained from the publisher or author.

ISBN: 978-1-68396-433-9
LIBRARY OF CONGRESS CONTROL NUMBER: 2020948305
FIRST FANTAGRAPHICS BOOKS EDITION: June 2021
PRINTED IN China

3 2529 15026 5643

8-21